THE W COUNTRY AT WAR

AT WAR

REMINISCENCES FROM REFUGEES, EVACUEES AND THE HOME FRONT

EDITED BY

Lucinda Hersey & Catherine Mason

Broadcast
BOOKS

This book is produced in collaboration with BBC Radio Bristol and Somerset Sound, and is the inspiration for Radio Bristol's series, "The West Country at War" (produced by Peter Lawrence) first broadcast to commemorate the 50th anniversary of V.E. Day in May 1995.

Text © 1995 by Broadcast Books,
4 Cotham Vale
Bristol BS6 6HR

Design by Ed Crewe

Printed by Bath Press, Avon.

isbn: 1 8740902 71 0

Cover Painting: **Fire Guard at Weston-Super-Mare**
by Barry Craig c. 1942
Reproduced by kind permission of
Bristol Museums and Art Gallery.

ACKNOWLEDGMENTS

This book would not have been possible without the generosity of the people of the South West, who responded in their hundreds to appeals over BBC Radio Bristol for personal war stories. Many have entrusted us with the photographic material reproduced here – war mementoes which had been carefully kept for fifty years. We would like to thank them all, and apologise to those whose stories we have not managed to include here, for reasons of space.

Special thanks are due to Gillian Heath, who gave unstintingly of her time to interview, transcribe and edit many of the accounts in this book, Caroline Hurst for help with the transcripts, and to Geoff Collard.

We would also like to thank Pete Lawrence and Vicky Klein of BBC Radio Bristol for putting so much of their archive material at our disposal, Monsignor Gabriel Leyden and Eve Levin for helping to publicise our appeals to the Catholic and Jewish communities of the region, and Clifton College in Bristol for helping us to track down staff at the college during the war. Finally, David Goodland most generously helped us to transcribe his interviews with American GIs. His play The Life and Death of a Buffalo Soldier is based on his extensive researches into the experiences of GIs in the South West during the war. At the time of writing *The Life and Death of a Buffalo Soldier* is being premiered at the Bristol Old Vic.

PICTURE CREDITS

DENNIS McHARRIE
LUCK

I suppose they'll say his last thoughts were of simple things
Of April back at home, and the late sun on his wings;
Or that he murmured someone's name
As earth reclaimed him sheathed in flame.
Oh God! Let's have no more of empty words,
Lip service ornamenting death!
The worms don't spare the hero;
Nor can children feed upon resounding praises of his deed.
'He died who loved to live,' they'll say,
'Unselfishly so we might have today!'
Like hell! He fought because he had to fight;
He died that's all. It was his unlucky night.

(Reproduced by kind permission of the Oasis Trust)

INTRODUCTION

We were asked by BBC Radio Bristol to put together a book to accompany their series of war reminiscences to commemorate the 50th anniversary of VE Day. Our most daunting questions were: how would we set about finding a wide enough variety of reminiscences which would give some sense of what war was like for people in the South West, what should be included, and where should we draw the limits? For practical reasons, we soon realised that our best approach would be to record accounts of the war as experienced by people who lived in the South West, or who arrived here from abroad during that time. We are not offering a factual account of wartime events in the South West, or the experiences of those who left the region to fight abroad.

Radio Bristol broadcast an appeal for people to write or phone in with their war experiences. This they did in their hundreds, often sending in precious and irreplaceable photographs. Many of these accounts centred around the terrible shared experience of the Blitz, or being sent as evacuees to the safety of Somerset, Devon and Cornwall. A good selection of these stories are included here.

We began to dig a little harder. Where were the conscientious objectors? The Prisoners of War? The refugees? The GIs? We asked everyone about their relations' wartime experiences: our local greengrocer, the butcher, the newsagent, the owners of the Italian restaurant, Mr Jewell of Betterware, the babysitters. We put notices up in libraries and churches. We quickly became terrible pests, buttonholing all our friends with questions about wartime relatives until their eyes glazed and they made excuses about having to dash. But one contact led to another, and very gradually, the most moving and fascinating stories were drawn out of people who in some cases had not talked about their wartime experiences for decades.

The survivors of that wartime generation are the grandparents of today; they were children or young adults fifty years ago. Our enquiries triggered many emotional memories: of the waste of war, of children being separated from parents, and husbands and wives from each other, and of so much death and injury – both mental and physical. There were also many happier recollections of courting and wartime romances, and of the solidarity of lives sharing the daily realities of air-raid shelters and rationing. Some deeply regretted what they did under the pressures of the moment, some were still gripped with bitterness at what they had endured, while some felt that the war was in many ways the best time of their lives. But what was astonishing for us was the extent to which those interviewed took pains to make their accounts as scrupulously accurate as they could, and their judgements as fair as hindsight could make them. This was especially noticeable with those who perhaps had suffered most: the refugees from Europe.

Overwhelmingly, we had an impression of men and women who had been tempered by an ordeal that had bound them all together. While some felt grimly satisfied that Germany had also suffered the devastation of widespread bombing and hunger, especially at the end of the war, many others would not, in retrospect, have wished their experiences on other people like themselves. It is certainly not as a result of selective editing that the reader will find triumphalism and flag-waving noticeably absent from these accounts.

Why did the interviewees talk to us so candidly and generously? Perhaps because an archive like this is a last chance to pass on to children and grandchildren the experiences that moulded their lives. Those who were old or middle aged when the war started in 1939 have already died – these are the last memories we have of a world war that, we all desperately hope, will never happen again.

The qualities of courage, humour and modesty shine through these quiet accounts of extraordinary lives. It has been a revelation and a pleasure to us to interview everyone in this book, and we hope that their voices will now find the audience they deserve.

CONTENTS

CHAPTER 1

THE START OF WAR AND THE BLITZ

———

FRANK BUCKLEY

I'd spent the night before the outbreak of war at what was the ARP control centre which had been established as an AFS depot (Auxillary Fire Station). It was actually Lefevre's garage up at Filton, Northville. I'd spent the night on a camp bed there, as we thought something was going to blow up, and so we listened at 11.15 to the broadcast. It was a big empty garage, with three or four fire engines in it (they'd converted some ambulances from Shield's Laundry) and the pumps all around us. We sat around in a big circle, in chairs. The drivers were a couple of girl ambulance drivers, and we were waiting.

We had a single telephone there, that was all. Previously I'd sounded the siren for a public test – we had a siren control switch. So I sounded the siren again, the Alert, almost immediately after the broadcast.

I'd gone over to Germany in 1936, for a holiday in Berlin, and stayed most of the summer there. This was the old Berlin of Cabaret and all that – then in 1938 I did a long cycle tour down the Rhine and into the Black Forest, staying at youth hostels. There I mixed with the Hitler Youth and the Brown Shirts, and they of course were boasting that the war was brewing, so I came over and joined Civil Defence. The Germans were only supposed to have gliders, but of course Goebbels was building aircraft. And they were talking about submarines, and you don't have submarines for peacetime traffic!

I had already taken a controllers and instructors course, and we were setting up the control centres. I'd helped to set up the wardens' posts in Filton, and they'd asked me to come down into Bristol, where I was setting up the wardens' posts with the police. I was reading all the ARP circulars for civil defence, and in Bristol we got a handbook for wardens, so I was well in the midst of it. We were taking it quite seriously, digging trenches all over Filton, filling the sand bags, and of course we'd already issued the gas masks. I went around all the schools issuing them. But I don't think there was a general anticipation of war. The previous year we'd had the Munich crisis, when nothing happened, so I think a lot of people thought it was going to fizzle out.

The older generation thought it was going to be fought with gas, but over in Germany I'd rather had the impression that it was going to be a fire raid and an HE raid (high explosives). We'd had the dummy run, you might say, of Hitler in Spain, and I'd seen the reports and talked with the people there. Most of the trouble was caused by incendiary bombs dropped from aircraft, and no gas was used. Quite frankly, I'd always felt that as we were on the westward side of Europe, with prevailing winds towards the continent. No one was going to try and gas this side! So I went for training for the incendiary bomb, and we found that it was this that destroyed the shopping centre of Bristol.

I was moved down into Bristol, and I had a flat at the corner of Small St and Martin's Bank in Corn St. I also trained all the fire guards in that area, and we set up a system of control rooms at the tops of the buildings, where we had watching posts, and cat walks! We were able to go from every building, from the GPO to Martin's Bank and all over those commercial buildings in Corn St. We could also get to the incendiary bombs on the roofs.

The first raid I was in was on the 24th November, 1940 – that's when the whole of the shopping centre in Bristol went. I was at Martin's Bank, and they said they had a purple (telephone alarm) at the warden's bank, which was situated, by the way, at The Regent Cinema in Castle St. So I went over there, and at 6.15pm we had the alert, and sounded the sirens. Almost immediately afterwards there were waves of aircraft, and then the incendiaries started dropping. So that was the Real Thing. The whole of Corn St, Wine St and up through what is now the shopping centre of Bristol was covered with incendiary bombs. We started to fight the fires, but it was very difficult because although we had the fire service there we hadn't any water, because all the mains had gone. The river was well down and the pumps wouldn't lift the water. So at about midnight the fire chief pulled us all out, and I returned then to my watching post at the top of the building in Corn St, and went up on the roof there. The whole of the city was ablaze. The north had gone, up towards Park St – that was the night the museum went, and the Princess Cinema, there was trouble over in Bedminster – I could see this all around me.

MRS SPARROW

My father was twenty-five years in the police force in Bristol, and he retired in August 1939. My mother had always wanted to live in a house in the middle of a field so we moved to Portishead and he took a job as steward at the Portishead Golf Club, which is now the Hole-In-One pub. The first bombs to drop on the West of England were around Battery Point, near Portishead. There were three bombs dropped around there that dropped in the mud. My sister and I were in twin beds in our room and I woke up and said, "There's a Jerry plane" and she said, "Oh rubbish, you've never heard a Jerry plane in your life." But you could tell by the drone of the engine. Then we heard these bombs whipping down, and there's me ducking under the bedclothes saying, "Oh Jesus, oh Christ." Then there was a silence and then my mother rushed out wondering what on earth was going on. My father was up at the golf club. This was before the home guard started, I think they called it the RVA and he was up there with a double barrelled shot gun. He came rushing down and said, "Mother! Jerry's over here bombing us!" and she said, very dramatically, "Daddy, line us all up against the wall and shoot us now!"

She soon got fed up with living in the middle of a field (the cottage was on the top of the cliff by the Hole-In-One). She had forgotten that my brother, sister and I were all at work in the middle of Bristol and she was alone all day. My Dad then took over the Swan Hotel in Stokes Croft, Bristol. It was August of September 1940 and we were there when the blitz started. The first raid blew all the windows out and my Dad then decided in his wisdom that the bar in the back of the pub, which was half underground, was safe enough for shelter.

Well the next raid blew the window in, so he told me and my brother to get up and fetch some blankets as we were going down to the cellar to shelter in there. So my brother and I dashed up round the circular staircase at the Swan Hotel to the bedrooms, where we grabbed all the pillows and blankets and threw them down the stairwell. We went down into the cellar and I said to John, "We hadn't better put these straight on the floor", so we got the empty crates of beer bottles and formed them into roughly the size of a double bed and we put an eiderdown on the top of that, pillows on the top and blankets and it looked quite comfortable until you lay on it. We had two Londoners staying with us then and in the middle of all this, Mabel, in a very cockney voice, said "I've slept in some places in my time, but this is the first time I've 'ad the neck of a bottle straight up me arse!"

When the first raid was over I felt a bit claustrophobic and I said to my Dad, "Can I go out and get some fresh air?" He said I could as long as John went with me, so we walked down Stokes Croft. When we got to the bottom, all the fire engines were there, as that was when the centre of Bristol was most severely damaged. Just down below the hotel, there was a gents' outfitters shop and when we'd passed it we'd noticed that the window had been blown out. The window was absolutely crammed full with shirts and ties and trilbies and all the things that men wear. We were gone ten minutes, maybe quarter of an hour but no longer, and we came back and went indoors. Shortly afterwards a police sergeant called round and said, "I saw your daughter out for a walk just now. Did they notice anybody by the gents shop?" We said, "No, we didn't notice anybody at all." In the time that we had walked down Stokes Croft and walked back again, somebody had stolen every scrap out of that window. We didn't see a soul.

On another occasion we had an unexploded bomb at the back of the hotel. That blew an Anderson shelter out of the ground and it came down upside down, through the roof and on to the billiard table. It was completely intact, just upside down. As this bomb hadn't exploded, the police evacuated all the houses and sent them in through our cellar. The son of the people at the post office was there, and when he came in my Mum asked him if he'd like to go back into the post office and rescue anything, provided the police gave him permission, as his Mum and Dad were away. She thought perhaps he should try and get some of his Mum's treasures out. Anyway, he agreed and Dad went with him and got the police to let him go in to the post office. When he came out he'd only bought two things, which in his opinion were the things his mum would treasure most. There was the family bible, a great big one with brass clasps, and her fur coat. Of all the things in the post office, those were the two things he thought most valuable.

When it was the daylight raid on Filton, Dad called me out to the door of the Swan and he said, "Have a look at this." All these planes were going across and we thought in our ignorance that they were our planes. They were going over in mass formation. It wasn't very long afterwards before we saw farm carts and cars, lorries and everything bringing casualties down to the Royal Infirmary from the raid on the Rodney works.

Another time my Dad called me at night to see a plane caught in three searchlights, and as I got to the door and looked up, the bomb doors opened and this stream of bombs came falling out. I just dashed down to the cellar. Now my Dad always kept a huge great bungalow bath full of water at the bottom of the cellar steps in case the water was ever cut off. We'd have some down there that we could boil and use if it came to it. Well, I knew the bath of water was there, my brother knew the bath of water was there, but the bloke behind me didn't and he went headfirst into it.

There was a rubber factory straight opposite the Swan hotel and one day that had an oil bomb dropped on it, so it caught fire. Close by, on the corner of Stokes Croft and Ashley Road, there was a big grocery shop. While the fire was raging, my brother put his elbow into the glass door and opened the lock and we went in there. At that time tea used to come loose in great big chests and four of us got these great big tea chests out on to the road and we rolled out whole wheels of cheese and everything else that was in large packets that we could move out from the shop. When the fire was under control and everything was all right, we helped put everything back in the shop and went home. I said to Mum, "I'd love a cup of tea", as we'd just lifted all these tea chests backwards and forwards out there. And it turned out we hadn't so much as a leaf of tea in the whole house.

We had a tiny little yard at the back of the hotel, and my Dad used to have us out there practically daily, working the stirrup pump. He'd say, "If ever we have a fire, nobody's to lose their head. You must be cool, calm and collected." On every floor in the place he had baths of water and buckets of sand and he'd tell us that as long as we didn't panic, there'd be no need to send for the NFS(National fire Service). So we were there one night and incendiary bombs were dropping everywhere. Suddenly we heard some glass break. We had three skylights in the place, so we went round checking them all and at one we found a pile of broken pieces. We went upstairs to check all the rooms and when we got to my mother's bedroom, it was on fire from end to end. We closed the door and dashed down to Dad and said, "Quick, stirrup pumps,

Mum's bedroom's on fire!" There was a big wide passage at the Swan Hotel and my father became like a raging lunatic. I'd never heard him use a bad word up until then, but there he was storming up and down the passageway saying, "The best bloody room in the house and it's burning!" and we had to send for the NFS to put the fire out. Unfortunately we kept all the best things in my mother's room including the family photographs and of course we lost the lot.

LILIAN DOUGLAS

When Chamberlain came back with that piece of paper, saying "Peace In Our Time", nobody really believed him, because immediately after he said that, the munitions factories went on full-time and over-time production. Gradually we were all geared up for war. We had air-raid shelters, and then we were issued with gas masks. I put mine on once, I suppose... it was particularly trying for the children, because they had to take them to school. I had two little ones, aged four and seven. It was a terrible time. It really was a terrible time. I adored my children. My parents died before I got married, when I was quite young, so I only had my immediate family. My husband became a Special Constable; he was out most of the time. It was all terrifying. You didn't want it to happen, yet you could see it coming. It was inevitable. There was no way out, and the propaganda was geared to the fact that there definitely was going to be a war.

When I heard the announcement of war, I felt despair. I had lived through the previous war – I was four when that started, and I could still recall all that... We were all praying and hoping that the Germans wouldn't go into Poland, or that they would take their soldiers out, but they were portrayed as so uncaring, that we didn't expect it. But I didn't think it would last too long – everyone thought it would be over by Christmas. Now when I think back I hope that such a war will never, ever, happen again. I don't think wars should ever occur. Somehow other means must be found to have peace between countries – not war. In my opinion, it's a needless waste of life, and nothing is really solved, as in the last war, and the war before that. We were really the victims rather than the victors, because it took years to get over it, whereas the losers got on far better than we did, both times. So although we say we won the war, we lost.

MRS DUNFORD

*Gwen Dunford, on the right of the picture,
sitting on top of the Anderson shelter
in her back garden in Birmingham.*

I was born in Birmingham and lived in a district called Greet. It wasn't a large area, but there were lots of factories there including Brooke Tools, Serk, Wilder's Fireworks, Dudley and Lowe and the B.S.A. munitions factory. I think it might be the reason we had so much bombing.

I was fifteen when the raids first started. At night we automatically went down to the Anderson shelter because the air-raid warning would go in any case, every night. That went on for almost a year. We'd go down, my Mum, Dad, little brother and the dog, and we'd always have to sleep on those hard bunks, which I really hated. The snoring irritated me too and so sometimes I'd creep out to get back to my bed, but my Dad would soon come, yelling at me to get out of bed and come back to the shelter. It was always lovely to hear the all clear go the next morning. Of course it was too late to go to bed, you had to think about going to work. You'd see all the ruins, incendiaries and bombs that hadn't gone off on the way, so of course it took a long time to get to work anyway because the bus was held up so much. It affected your whole life. You were in the shelter every night – I was learning to dance and all sorts of other things and you couldn't go anywhere or do anything because of the raids.

Dad bought a little car and tried to persuade my mother to come to Frome, where he was born. She was born and bred in Birmingham and didn't want to leave all her friends and family behind.

The last three weeks we were in Birmingham, it was really bad. Dad was in the A.R.P. and was often out for many hours at night, putting out incendiary bombs and so on. I remember when Dudley & Lowe, which was a factory practically at the bottom of our garden, was on fire and we had to evacuate our shelter because the heat was so intense. We had to go cringing against the wall as we edged along in case we got hit by machine gun fire from the planes above. It's funny how you could always tell the sound of a German aircraft. Anyway, we finally made it to another shelter over the road where there were nine of us all sitting on the edge of the bunks, trying to keep our feet out of about ten inches of water on the shelter floor.

Dad said that under no circumstances was I to put my head out of the shelter to have a look, but of course I did when it was a bit quieter. There were fires raging all over the place, especially the B.S.A. ammunition factory. It was havoc on the bus journey to work next morning as well, as there were loads of ruins with firemen still trying to put out the flames. Fisher and Ludlow had gone, along with loads of other buildings and when I finally got into work in Lionel Street, there were firemen in my office squirting their hoses at the building opposite which was still on fire.

The last night we were in Birmingham was even worse. My Dad was out a very long time and my Mum found out he'd very nearly been killed by some shrapnel which had missed him by a fraction. Meanwhile part of our ceiling upstairs had collapsed onto the bed, and Mum was so upset by everything that she finally agreed to leave.

We left instantly, taking only the dog and an eiderdown and a very few personal things. We had a lovely home and we just left it, because nothing had been planned, and I had a good job with a firm of accountants and Dad had a good job, but we just left. We had to write for our cards from work when we got down to Frome.

I shall never forget that journey. We managed to get out of the town eventually after circuiting round seventeen unexploded bombs and numerous craters in the road and we went to see my grandparents and Dad's brother to say goodbye. They were staying temporarily at my Dad's uncle and aunt's house in Erdington on the outskirts of Birmingham, because they'd had all the windows blown out of their home in Saltley by a bomb and they were staying in Erdington while they were waiting their turn for replacements.

The journey coming down to Frome next day was memorable. Everyone was rationed with petrol and my Dad hadn't got enough petrol coupons to get all the way. We stopped in Kempsey over night and the driver of a big RAF lorry helped us out. The driver, who was called Fred, asked Dad if he could take me to a dance in Kempsey that evening and Dad had agreed, so I'd gone off to this dance with him earlier and then later, about midnight, Fred and Dad siphoned off enough petrol from the lorry to get down to Frome.

We finally got to Frome and I remember the joy of sleeping in a proper bed. I appreciated it so much I couldn't get over how wonderful it was. We stayed with relatives for six weeks and then we managed to get a little house of our own. I met my husband, who was actually my second cousin. He was in the home guard at that time because he was only seventeen.

Mrs. Dunford wearing her Auxiliary Fire Service uniform – she joined the service to be in Frome, though to her knowledge only one bomb fell in the town.

Dad did persuade someone to take him back up to Birmingham a few days after we got to Frome with a lorry to load up with furniture and everything, but the air-raid warning went after about half an hour, so he had to come away. He got a little bit, but nothing much. Everything was just left and the neighbours had it. Mum had a good neighbour, that's another reason she didn't want to leave and I think she had most of the things because my Dad didn't manage to go back again.

The saddest part of the story is that after we'd been here only about two weeks, there was a direct hit on the house in Erdington. My Dad had to go back to identify his parents, aunt and uncle, and his brother, but he couldn't because they'd been blown to bits. It had been a land mine, dropped by a returning bomber after a raid. My Dad never really got over it.

I went to the town hall in Birmingham a few years ago and was shown their names in a book in the Hall of Memories as civilians killed during the war.

MR BAKER

I was nineteen at the start of the war and I was working for the B.A.C. (British Aircraft Company), which was a reserved occupation, so I spent my formative years there.

The first time it really struck home that we were at war was when they introduced special lighting, or lack of it, on motor cars and other transport. That happened when we used to work shifts, those on the same shift as myself came on at two o'clock and finished at ten. On that particular day, everything was as usual coming to work as it was still daylight then, but when we came to go home, we weren't allowed to use a light, so

One of the hangars at B.A.C. during the war.

we had to drive home pretty well in the dark. It was quite a shock! It was a thing that people got used to soon enough, because less and less people were able to use their cars with petrol rationing and everything. You weren't able to get hold of petrol unless there was a really good reason for you to have it.

From then on things started to deteriorate. We found ourselves working longer and longer hours and working a seven day week. Everything was blacked out so you couldn't see the daylight and I remember it got terribly hot in the summer and very unpleasant and uncomfortable.

Then the air-raids began. First they raided the centre of Bristol, then there was a lull for a while. The government found that people were going into the shelters for too long a period. The warnings were sounded as soon as the aircraft came over the South coast, and we all rushed off down to the shelter and spent time playing cards or listening to gramophone records of Vera Lynn and Frank Sinatra. We spent an awful lot of time there considering the amount of time the aircraft were directly overhead. So they introduced a new system which gave you a much shorter warning time.

We had a daylight raid in September. The first air-raid warning came at six-thirty in the morning (we were on the morning shift, six until two). It lasted about half an hour but nothing happened. We heard an aeroplane but didn't see anything. Then we went to breakfast from nine to nine-thirty and just before nine-thirty the air-raid siren went again. It lasted about half an hour and again we didn't see anything. Then at about eleven o'clock, the air-raid siren sounded for a third time, and it was a glorious day so we all went off down to the shelters which were in the orchard gardens of the company. After about a quarter of an hour we realised it was getting a bit serious because bombs started dropping close by. It's the only time I've seen concrete swell with the shock of the blast. People who normally spent fine days on top of the shelter in the sunshine came shooting down to the little entrances. All the card games and record playing finished and we were just terrified for about ten minutes while all the bombs fell.

We were luckier than the Rolls Royce part of the factory which was then the engine division of B.A.C., where they'd hit some hangars down the bottom of the hill and one or two shelters were hit at the top of the hill, which unfortunately killed a lot of chaps who worked in our tool room. It was about half past two before any of us went home, by the time everything had calmed down a bit. All sorts of things came to light

A Luftwaffe photograph of Filton from Mr. Baker's collection.

afterwards, for example there was a barrage balloon operating from where the Rolls Royce school is now and there was a big horse in the field next to it, which nobody ever saw again. Also walking up the hill was a platoon of guardsmen who had no time to reach shelter and they suffered badly. There were about eighty people killed inside the works, and about a hundred outside, and all the bodies were taken into Filton church while things were sorted out.

The next day the air-raid siren went again at six-thirty in the morning and again at nine-thirty, mid-morning, but nothing happened. There was a very nervous peace for the rest of the day. Then the following day exactly the same thing happened and this

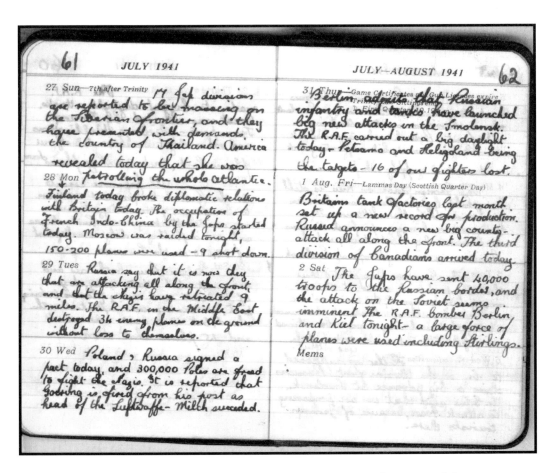

An extract from the diary kept by Mr. Baker, charting the course of the war.

time the bombers came. However, by this time a squadron of Hurricanes had been flown in, a Polish squadron, and just before the second air-raid warning went off on the third day, they took off and started making altitude very quickly. When the enemy aircraft came, they were met by the Hurricanes and only managed to drop a few bombs before they were driven back down to the south coast where another squadron near Southampton drove them nearly up to Bristol again. They lost quite a number of aircraft.

MRS PAT ELLWOOD

During the early years of the blitz on Bristol, I lived with my parents in West India House, next to the Sceptre pub on Bristol Bridge. My Dad was ex-navy and got called up early in 1940.

The first bomb I saw was soon after the war started and it fell on Mac Fisheries in Baldwin Street. It was some kind of fire bomb and when we heard it we rushed out to find the top of the building was ablaze. People were hanging their heads out of the windows, screaming for help. Dad tried frantically to knock the doors down but he couldn't do it in time and those poor people fell back in and were burned. My Dad was a kind man and he never really got over it. He kept saying "I just couldn't do anything."

After that he went into the navy, but on the day of the big blitz he was home on leave. He and my Mum had gone to Bedminster to have tea with my Auntie, and my friend Joan and I were left at home. We didn't want to go to Bedminster because we had a date with two boys that evening.

Joan and I were at the top of West India House when the sirens went and we saw these lights fall out of the sky. Later we learnt they were flares. The whole place was lit up and we were just watching and admiring when suddenly there were these terrific bangs and the buildings seemed to move. Picking up Joey, our budgie, in his cage, we went down to the basement shelter. On the way down we stopped to look out of the door to see if the boys had turned up and we saw there were fires all around us, so we hurried down to the shelter.

CHAPTER 1 – THE BLITZ

Then it really started and we heard the bombs rattling down in Bridge Street, Castle Street and Wine Street and we were beginning to get alarmed. Joey didn't like it much either. Then we heard a knock on the little door leading to Welsh Back. When we opened the door there were two air raid wardens standing outside. "Blimey, there's two kids in here!" one of them said. They were great, they got us out and took us and the budgie over to St. Nicholas Church crypt. There were an awful lot of people there already and we looked round to see if we could spot our two dates, but no such luck.

It sounded as though all hell had let loose outside, then somebody shouted, "Everybody out!" because a bomb had fallen on the church. We climbed out of the crypt and when we got outside, the wonderful A.R.P. man told us to follow him. It was then that we realised the horror of the whole thing. Buildings were down, fires were blazing, and there were bodies all around us. Amongst it all, suddenly my Dad appeared. He had walked from Bedminster to see if we were all right and didn't know if we would come out of the crypt or not. He said that from a distance it didn't look as if anybody would be alive in the centre of town. Then he told us to go with the warden while he stayed on to help, so Joan, me, and Joey set off with a crowd of others. We ran through Wine Street with the bombs still falling and about three quarters of us made it to the Council House where we stayed until the all clear.

The next morning the devastation was appalling and we really understood what the war meant. There were many such incidents afterwards, when we were turned out to sleep in church halls, classrooms and so on, until we moved out to a house in Kings Head Lane.

Thinking my mother was safe then, I joined up in the W.R.N.S. and waved goodbye to her at Temple Meads Station in September 1943. She was found dead in her bed on December 10th having died from a stroke at fifty-one, as much a victim of war as she would have been if a bomb had struck her. I never went back to live in Bristol after that.

LILIAN DAVIES

At the beginning of the war, I worked as a cook at the Bridge Hotel near Bristol Bridge and the job included accommodation. On the evening of 24th November 1940, I was preparing meals down in the kitchen, which was below pavement level.

I had just sent a welsh rarebit in the service lift up to the pantry above. When the next order was ready, I pulled the lift down and was surprised to see the same welsh rarebit

The ruin of The Dutch House on Wine Street which Lilian Davies saw burning as she ran past to seek shelter from the incendiary bombs.

was still in the lift. I called out, but nobody answered and I suddenly realised how quiet it was, except for a faint swishing sound.

Outside the kitchen was a passage with a door leading to a small walled courtyard. As I opened the door, I saw the whole sky was lit up by incendiary bombs and as they fell on the ground there was no sound but the swishing noise.

I slammed the door and ran up the stairs which led to the foyer of the hotel, which turned out to be completely deserted. I looked into some of the rooms hoping to find someone, then as I came out of the bar, a door on the other side of the foyer opened. It was the owner of the hotel, who shouted at me to get down to the cellar. He said he'd only just realised I was missing.

We stayed down in the cellar for a while until someone called us out because the hotel was well alight. We were to head for the crypt of St. Nicholas Church. Bridge Street was lit up with fires on both sides of the road and there were firemen and soldiers from Horfield Barracks trying to hose water onto the buildings. We all ran down the middle of the road towards the crypt, getting soaked with water from the hoses on the way.

We stayed in the crypt for only a short time before we were told to move on again as the roof of the church was on fire. We were to go to the Guildhall in Broad Street where the cellars were open as an air raid shelter. As we ran up High Street The Dutch House was on fire and a small band of men with hose pipes were doing their best to try and save the building. There was debris all over the road and a soldier was lying amid all the mess. We were being hurried along, but I think his injuries were serious.

We spent the rest of the night down in the cellars of the Guildhall, opposite the Grand Hotel. The cellar was made up of alcoves and recesses and in one of the recesses was a double bed made up for use. The shelter filled up with Grand Hotel staff and others; then the owners of the bed, who were local publicans, turned up in their dressing gowns and both promptly got into bed and went to sleep!

It was just after this that we learnt that the Bridge Hotel was gone forever. The only things I possessed were what I stood up in and so I cried for a long time that night, wondering what the future would be like.

We spent the night on the concrete floor and my clothes were still damp and dirty when the morning came. My boss was kind enough to to give me 10d to get a bus back to Bedminster where my mother lived. Then on the Tuesday morning I joined the crowds at the Labour Exchange, wearing begged and borrowed clothing and with not very much hope of success. We had to leave our names and addresses so we could be contacted in due time.

KATE LOTHIAN

If you were in town, and the siren went, you were shepherded to a shelter whether you wanted to or not, and you might stay there two or three hours. You wouldn't be let out until the All Clear went. We had a small Jack Russell, and even before the sirens went, the dog would move towards the under-stairs cupboard where we'd all go during the raids at the beginning of the war. Whenever he did that, we'd all look up and we'd say, the sirens are going! And the sirens did. We'd open the door and the dog was first in, on his bed, and we all went in after him. He could probably hear the aircraft – but he was always first in!

When I was on watch we used to stay up all night in a house in Claremont Rd, with the telephones manned, waiting for the Germans to land. And you would spend all night there – and nobody would ever phone you... I presumed that if they had done, we would phone the police – that is what we understood we would do – and they would take it on from there. We had no idea who we would be taking the call from; nobody really told you anything. It was all very cagey. You just sat there with the telephone, absolutely horrified, because you didn't know what you were going to do... I felt there were better things to do.

Then a group of us decided we would join the Women's Home Guard. Some of the work was done at the old Evening World Building, and some at the Cotham Grammar School. We were taught semaphore, with white flags, how to strip down a bren gun, and how to put a bayonet into a German soldier, with the In Twist Out action! But I rather felt that a very tall German in full uniform was hardly going to wait for my bayonet...

CHAPTER 1 – THE BLITZ

We were sent to the centre of Bristol, where the bombed buildings were, and were given fire drill. First of all, we were to see an incendiary bomb. We would go through a little smoke with our gas mask on, to look at the bomb. It wasn't very big, but it sizzled like a firework – it frightened us all to death. And we went out at the other side, thinking – what ever shall I do if I have to put one out? Then we went to an old building in Broadmead, and were taught to use the fire hoses, which were very big and strong. We were shown how to hold them until somebody mentioned the word "water!" At that point somebody shot water through the hoses, and we little women fell flat on our backs, covered in water, because we just didn't have the strength to hold the hose! I felt this was all a little bit beyond us women, but it was great fun because you had a comradeship with everybody.

One of the worst things when you were fire-watching was when you were sitting in your shelter under the stairs – if it wasn't our turn to go out – and you could hear the bombs dropping. You could hear them coming, which is quite awe-inspiring. You could tell they were getting nearer, because they were getting louder. You counted them... one, two, three, four, five ... and then, horrified, you thought, where is the sixth one going to fall? And if it went past you, you thought – my luck's in.

It was the saddest of times, as far as I was concerned, when people's houses got hit. I worked for the District Valuer's office, and we processed the claims. After the first bombing, the people all came in. We were as inadequate as they were... it was our first time, and in they came. They were shocked, and tired, and full of sadness because they had lost everything. Between us we just had to try and give them advice as to where they could go. As time went on you learned to cope, but the effort of dealing with this queue of people coming into the office on the first day after the raids was very very sad.

MR WEBB

Before the war I helped to assemble gas masks. We did this in the Fry's chocolate factory, which was then empty because they'd moved. It was in the Pithay, in Bristol. We assembled thousands of them at the end of '38 beginning of '39. They used scouts, boys brigade, and various organisations like that to assemble the masks. It was voluntary labour of course but I used to work for love in those days!

We used to go every evening after school to assemble these things, and at weekends. We assembled both the normal type of gas mask and those others that they used to put babies in as well.

Civil Defence Messenger Service, Central Control Bristol – 1940/41

CHAPTER 1 — THE BLITZ

When the war started, the scouts came under the direction of a Mr Freddie Ford, who was then a scout commissioner in Bristol. He organised the messenger service using the scouts and Boys Brigade, people who had bikes. We were attached to the various control centres. I was attached to the Bedminster control centre, then I was moved to the central control centre which was in Broadmead. Our job was that when the phones got broken, we just had to get on our bikes and pedal through the blitz to take these messages. Also when they were calling up reserves of ambulances and fire engines we used to have to cycle out from Broadmead to Ashton Gate or Bedminster Down to meet a convoy of ambulances and then take them to where they were required in Bristol. So we had to take them across Bristol in the middle of the blitz with all the muck coming down on us. I took one convoy from Ashton Gate to an orphanage for example, so we had some exciting times.

Some of the things we used to get up to were amazing. Every so often you'd get a shower of incendiary bombs come down and a lot of them didn't go off. We used to collect the ones that didn't go off in our saddle-bags and then take them back to our scout headquarters, empty them out and sell them for a shilling. There'd be an explosive thing in one end and there was this magnesium, which was the stuff that burnt.

One of the hazards that you encountered cycling through the blitz, with the anti air-craft guns exploding, was shrapnel coming down like rain sometimes. Shrapnel could cause very serious injuries. I was on Bristol Bridge when the first blitz started. We had a floating headquarters there for the sea scouts and we were out rowing on the harbour that night when at about six o'clock the flares started coming down. We had to get the younger members back home and then we went on duty. Being based in Broadmead of course the whole of that area was wiped out that night.

We did a lot of fire-watching, and where you worked in the various offices you had to do a duty fire-watch. I was working in Baldwin Street then so I used to do my fire-watching down there.

The central control headquarters of the civil defence for Bristol was based in Broadmead and then we had a reserve unit which was under the base of the university tower. We had a team up there in case Broadmead got wiped out, so that we could carry on operating from there. When Broadmead got eventually wiped out, the central control moved to Badminton Girls' School. The girls had been evacuated of course.

Mr. Webb's Civil Defence Messenger Service certificate.

We carried on right through the blitz doing these various things. I used to cycle all over the place. It kept us very fit. Sometimes we had to take part in some of the rescues, where people were trapped in buildings. I was seventeen then and so I learnt a lot about life very quickly. Some of the incidents were dreadful. Some were quite funny – we saved a vicarage once and the vicar gave me ten shillings. About a fortnight later his church was burnt so I sent it back.

So the scouts were actually a strong part of the civil defence, or ARP (air raid precautions) as it was formally known.

CANON KELLY

I was in Salisbury at the time of Dunkirk, and I saw the soldiers that had been evacuated come back in the lorries, in just what they stood up in – shirt and trousers. Without any equipment – literally nothing. But the extraordinary thing was their feeling of resilience – you'd think we'd won the war, despite the destruction of the whole army! It was a tremendous escape. It must have been the intervention of God, that they got out alive.

I remember listening to Churchill's speech, when it really seemed that we were losing the war. And this speech, so dramatic in its effect, opened the whole future up, so that you felt the war couldn't be lost. There was no doubt that Churchill had this tremendous charisma.

I was transferred from Salisbury to Bath in 1940 – on 12th July, a date of great significance to an Irishman! I was on the train and the conductor came along and announced an air raid alert – although what he thought we could do about it, I don't know! But in that first year at Bath, there were between 300 – 400 air raid alerts. We were so close to Bristol, only ten miles across the valley, that every time the planes came across for Bristol, we had an alert in Bath.

The night the church was hit I slept through the alert, because we'd had a raid the previous night. Somebody had to come and call me, even though the siren was just on the corner of the building! We had become so blase about alerts, that even though we'd had one attack, it didn't really register as something terrible. In that raid we had a very bad time. I can remember vividly hearing the bombers going out, and then turning to come in for their run, and then the bombs being released. We had a direct hit on the presbytery – a big three-storey building, with a basement – and we had heard the whirr of this bomb coming down. A priest and I were watching for incendiaries at a presbytery window that looked out onto the back, and onto the roof of the church. He was standing at the window, and I was standing beside him, just clear of a cross passage that ran between us from the presbytery into the church. When the bomb hit, the top two stories of the building caved in, and the priest next to me vanished with the rubble into the basement. My tin hat was peppered with glass from the window, but I had been sheltered from the collapse by the porch of the passage. A woman and her daughter who had come in for shelter had thought the basement would be the safest place, and they were also buried.

We had a fire fighting team, made up of a very big contingent of Irishmen who were working at an underground munitions factory, built by MacAlpine, at Corsham. Many of them were lodging at Bath. They had a bad reputation for drinking and rowdy behaviour, yet a number of them used to come to St John's to worship... It was in fact an extraordinary sight, because the church holds 500, but when they came we had to find extra chairs. It was a tremendous congregation of big men! The parish priest and an Irishman who had also been looking out for incendiaries came running around to the front of the church. They saw the total destruction, and couldn't believe that anyone would still be alive. The priest called out "Anybody there?" And he told me of his great relief when I answered "yes..." The Irishman with the priest was called Jim McLaughlin, from Donegal. He'd been lodging nearby, and his house had been destroyed during the first night of the raids. He had a sister working in Swindon, and had come down to the railway station to stay with her for the night. But then it had occurred to him that there might not be enough fire watchers, and he left the platform and came down to us. It really should go into the record, what he did. He was a steel erector, and I think the strongest man I ever met. We wanted to try and find Father Sheridan who had been buried, and the people in the basement. We came down the stairs to the basement, and at the bottom was a door blocked by the debris. Jim literally took the door apart in his hands. Within about half an hour we had found Father Sheridan buried, and dead, of course. We realised that the mother and daughter sheltering in the basement kitchen were dead as well.

We really didn't know what to do, and thought that we should tell the police – although what we expected the police to do, I don't know. The raid was still on. I went into the police station and met this young policeman, and told him the situation. He said, "Well, I'll have to have that in writing!" So I said he'd have to put up with just a verbal report... Then he saw I was bleeding from a little cut in my leg, and said I'd have to go into hospital for an anti-tetanus injection. I said I'd just escaped with my life and would take my chances...

I went back and we stood in the forecourt of the church, watching the planes firing tracer bullets. We thought they were ours, but discovered later that they were German planes. Next day they found one man with his head cut clean off by bullets. What had misled us was the fact that there was a night-fighter station out at Colerne, and we thought that our planes had taken off. But it happened that that weekend there was a transfer of personnel, and there was nobody there. Bath had no anti-aircraft cover that night, so the German planes had an uninterrupted time of it, and strafed the place. That was 27th April, 1942.

Exactly a year later, on 26th April, I remembered in my mass the people who had lost their lives on that anniversary. That night before going to bed I was thinking about the blitz, and I later woke up with a nightmare. I looked at my watch, and it was ten to two, which was the exact time that the bomb had struck. We knew that was the time, because the church clock in the tower had stopped at exactly that time, and stood at ten to two for a couple of years. That was eerie...

The bombing brought the priests and the people closer together. The bomb had taken the roof off the church, so where were we going to hold our services? Now in the First World War, the convent built some temporary classrooms. And because Bath was subject to floods at that time, with the waters reaching the convent, these temporary classrooms were put on stilts – seven feet high. And this created an enormous space underneath, which became what we called our "basilica" where we had mass. By the following Sunday after the Blitz this area had been organised. It was interesting for the priest because there were no walls, and you would be bellowing to be heard by those at the edges of the area, while those in front were deafened! In the following weeks we closed this area in with timber, and this became our church for at least 12 months.

The priest appealed to the Irishmen at mass to come and clear out the masonry which had fallen into the church. There were about 100 of them that set to work after mass – some of them didn't even bother to go home and change. They came in their Sunday best! And they worked until dark, and the following day as well – they took the day off work. They stacked the stones in the forecourt. Afterwards, when the firm came to repair the church and looked at what had been done, they said it would have taken them six weeks, with all their resources, to do what those Irishmen had done in a few days. This had a very interesting consequence. There was no building allowed during the war, but when the authorities came to inspect the damage, and saw the work that had been done by volunteers, they said, "These people deserve to have their church." And we were allowed to re-roof it, even during the war.

It was a time of great fervour, I would say, because in times of crisis we were made aware of our limitations. But we weren't really aware of what Catholics and Protestants in Germany were going through. There were a number of bishops in Germany – Galen of Munster was one – who did stand out against the Nazis, but one would have to say that there doesn't seem to have been any kind of revolt. But in England there wasn't really the awareness of how evil the Nazis were, there really seemed to be an ignorance about it. I don't remember it as an issue that occupied our attention. I think it was a revelation to the Germans as well as to the English when they discovered Dachau and Belsen after the war.

The bombing of Dresden shocked people, but I must be honest and and say that whatever our private prayers, that certainly wasn't something we publicly prayed about.

JOHN BUDD

I was six years old in 1939 when war was declared. I lived then in Catherine Mead Street, off Dean Lane in Bedminster and I went to St Paul's Infant School in Dean Lane. I clearly remember the morning in September when Prime Minister Chamberlain made his famous announcement. All the neighbours were in their tiny back gardens and the boy next door gave a great cheer when he heard the news. His father felled him immediately. Memories of the Great War were still very fresh.

All the preparations were made but nothing happened for a year. Two brick shelters were built at the Wills' factory end of Catherine Mead Street and some shelters were built in the school playground. We all had gas masks and had to carry them everywhere. We also had to carry a box of 'iron rations' in case we ended up in an air raid shelter with no food. My iron rations were in an Oxo tin and usually comprised some sandwiches and anything not on ration or in short supply.

Static water tanks were placed where the Fire Brigade had easy access. These tanks could be large circular metal ones or small canvas ones. There were two lots of firemen, the Auxiliary Fire Service (A.F.S.) who were part timers and the National Fire Service (N.F.S.) who were regulars.

For a time at the beginning of the war many schools were closed. I remember that all the kids had to collect in each others' front rooms while a teacher went the rounds and taught us all in rotation for an hour or two at a time.

My father had made his own preparations in our tiny, two-up two-down house. We were told the safest place in the house was the understairs cupboard, so my father cleared out the coal which we used to keep there and put in some chairs, some food and a cot for my baby brother. Then we waited for the air raid siren. I'm fifty-seven years old now but I and millions like me will never forget the sound of the siren. It scared us stiff. I still hate the Germans for that alone. Nothing much happened for about a year, but we had several false alarms.

Then one Sunday night in November 1940, we had our first full scale air raid. The sirens went off and petrified us. My mother grabbed the baby, and my father rushed my younger brother and me into our pitiful stair cupboard protection and locked the flimsy wooden door. Even I wondered how that was ever going to save us. We sat and listened to the sound of aircraft engines overhead and the ack-ack (anti aircraft) guns starting. Our own guns went off like crackers and were easy to pick out from the explosions of the German bombs, which burst with a deep "crump". If they landed near enough, they shook the whole house. My parents began to talk in loud voices about anything they could think of, just to try and drown the noise of the bombs and the guns and the shrieks of neighbours in the street who perhaps had lost a member of the family in the darkness.

My family were deeply religious and my father made us sing hymns at the tops of our voices. I clearly remember singing "Sun of my Soul, Thou Saviour Dear" and "Now the Day is Over" while bombs which were aimed at the Wills' factory rained down all around us. The factory was turning out munitions, which made it a target. Sometimes there was a lull and we waited for the all clear siren. But these pauses were only short breaks while a fresh wave of bombers arrived and gave us another dose while we sang our hearts out and our parents tried to stay brave. They didn't feel brave and we knew it. Don't blame my generation for hating the Germans; to us it goes deeper than putting towels on the best sunbeds.

At last the all clear siren went and the A.R.P. wardens rushed around blowing their whistles to tell us it was safe to come out. But some people never came out again. Where their houses had been there were now big gaps like teeth which had been pulled out. There was smoke everywhere and the smell of gas where gas mains had been fractured. Roads were impassable until they were cleared of debris.

My mother's sister lived a mile away in British Road and my father and I walked there to see if they were all right. I shall never forget that journey early in the morning. Firemen were still playing hoses on smouldering buildings and people were sorting through piles of furniture to see what could be saved. A car had been blown onto the roof of a building and hung there as though it would fall off any minute. Shops were boarded up and some of them had signs chalked up saying "Open for business". And the roads were full of people like us, walking to see if their friends or relatives had survived the terror of the night.

Later we all used the brick air raid shelter. Raids were so frequent now that we didn't wait any more for the sirens. We made the shelters our night homes and we went there as a matter of routine. The shelters contained rough bunks and we had to provide the bedding. The kids were given the best places to sleep and at times it was quite an adventure. Everybody helped everybody else – the feeling of comradeship was absolutely incredible.

I can still remember the condensation streaming down the walls and the smell of the smoking paraffin lamps that provided light and a little heat. At the height of a raid, everybody would sing songs and the adults would lean over the kids to protect them with their bodies in case there was a direct hit. There were two shelters in our street and they were back to back. Outside the one we didn't use, a canvas water tank was sited. One night a bomb landed on the tank which 'drowned' the bomb. Its presence saved a few lives because several people were killed or injured during the raid that night, both shelters being useless. I recall a warden whispering to my father that somebody's house had been destroyed, " but don't tell her till the morning".

We couldn't use the shelters so all the local population began to use the crypt of St Paul's Church in Coronation Road. Every night we went there at six in the evening and returned home at six in the morning. And for most of that time we were under attack. My brother and I, sent on ahead with our pyjamas on under our coats, stood hand-in-hand and watched as a plane came towards us with pretty lights bursting from its wings. An air raid warden screamed at us and threw us onto the ground, as we were being machine-gunned by a German pilot.

And so it went on until we were inevitably 'bombed out' and were given a council house in Lynton Road. We got there in time for the Good Friday Blitz, which nobody who survived it will ever forget. By now my father had been called up and my mother was looking after four young boys, all alone, with me the eldest at eight years old. We had an Anderson shelter in the garden, but that night we didn't bother to use it. We were quite sure we were goners.

I remember my mother driving us all, like a flock of sheep, under the kitchen table. She leaned over the top and prayed until she wept. Two land mines fell in our street and killed people we knew, and incendiary bombs came down like a hailstorm. Most of all, I remember the Germans' special wheeze for terrifying the population. They attached flights to their bombs which made them scream as they hurtled down. The effect made them sound like all the devils of hell let loose at once. We could hear them coming rapidly nearer and getting louder until we were sure they were headed for us, then they would explode nearby and the plaster would fall off the ceiling and we breathed again.

That was the last of the big raids. We collected shrapnel in boxes and looked for the flights of incendiary bombs – but they were so common that you didn't even bother to show anybody if you found one. A small boy can find adventure in most situations; when they brought the sand to make sandbags and piled it in a huge heap in Charlotte Street, we were delirious with joy. There were mountains of it, more than at Weston, and we dived in it, dug it, fell about in it and had a glorious time! And I've never since then experienced the kindness and tolerance and comradeship that everyone showed to each other when the news got worse and the bombs rained down.

And, very probably, the hatred felt by those around me for the Germans, who in their living memory had started two dreadful wars, rubbed off on me for all time. But I don't make the slightest apology for it.

CHAPTER 2

WAR WORK

MR BAKER

Although I worked at the B.A.C., I didn't join their Home Guard, I joined the one in Clifton where I lived. We started off with our headquarters being at the Bristol Zoo and the pitiful amount of ammunition we had was stored in the polar bear pit. There weren't any polar bears in there at the time! Then we moved to a strip club in Worrall Road, though there was no stripping going on. We missed that too! Then we

Mr. Baker's B.A.C. air raid shelter card

moved into Upper Belgrave Road, behind Worrall Road, looking towards the Downs. We were a machine gun platoon, unlikely as it might seem, and we had some American Browning machine guns and a tiny amount of ammunition.

As things developed during the war, the Americans turned up, and many of them were in Clifton College and several of the larger houses around the same area. They spent quite a bit of time trying to get to know you and seemed desperately keen to be liked, so they issued us with a challenge, rifle shooting, which took place at the Royal Fort. When these chaps turned up we had the shock of our lives because there we were with our ill-fitting air raid suits and they turned up in these beautiful uniforms and all with big medallions dangling down from their chests, first class sharp shooters and that kind of thing. Anyhow, we shot against them at the Royal Fort and beat them out of sight. It made the front page of the *Evening Post* at the time, but we never got our return match as we never saw them again! That was in about 1942.

A bit later we built our own rifle range, because we were a machine gun platoon, with these heavy half inch Brownings. Anyway, ammunition has a shelf life, and it becomes dangerous when it goes beyond it, so you have to get rid of it. You get told by whoever's in charge that the ammunition is duff and to shoot it away if possible. Well, we had nowhere to shoot it away, so we built a rifle range between Severn Beach and Avonmouth. It took us ages to do it, but we eventually completed it and we had quite a bit of ammunition by then, so we all went down there one Sunday morning. We had plenty of transport because there were three people in the platoon , two officers and one soon to be an officer, who were all in the car business! The Chrysler agent was one I remember. We had no trouble with petrol, strangely enough!

It was a glorious day that Sunday and we set up the machine guns. We started firing off at targets out towards the sea, and it wasn't for a good half hour that we suddenly realised that a tug pulling two barges was going down the river and the chap pulling the barges was dancing up and down because although we were hitting the targets with the majority of the bullets, some of them were going straight through and straight on and they were really putting the wind up him!

In the years when our Country

was in mortal danger

KENNETH EDWARD THOMAS BAKER

who served 23 March 1942 – 31 December 1944

gave generously of his time and

powers to make himself ready

for her defence by force of arms

and with his life if need be.

George R.I.

THE HOME GUARD

Mr. Baker's Home Guard Certificate.

ARTHUR LEEK

Working as a fireman it was so cold that water froze in the hoses. The turntable ladders were up at the general Hospital, and they were up there for four days; we couldn't get them down on account of the ice. And it was a bit distressing to knock off hose, only to find that you had to cut the hose off up the ladder because it was frozen solid! A lady went off to the canteen for a cup of tea and a tot of rum – that kept us going, but the foreman had to do quite a bit of walking to find out where she was!

It was all volunteers – quite a few of the regulars had already left Bristol for hired posts. Some had come in when volunteers were asked for, in 1937, and they were pretty well equipped. They'd had quite a bit of training, but these were fires that the regulars had never seen the like of before. We had told them what to do – going into buildings and putting out fires where they could, but when it actually happened, all they could do was stop the fires from spreading elsewhere – there was no going into the buildings. For example, one night we had a council house going, and a general post office: all over the place, as far as you could see, all you could see was fire. Well, you had to put out what you thought best at the time.

One night we had a raid – I think it was the night it was so freezing. One thing about the AFS at that time was that when the raids came along it used to amaze me that over ninety percent of the part-timers used to turn up. Of course all this applied to the women as well. There were women in control of the firemen, and in Avonmouth there were two of our girls who used to turn up regularly to man the control room. As soon as the sirens went they used to get on their bikes and ride to Avonmouth.

Well, I don't think they wanted recognition for what they did during the war. They were all doing a job, and I've never heard anyone express any wish to have a medal, or anything like that. It was furthest from their thoughts. There were quite a few characters – the board down at HQ now shows the list of people killed at Bristol belonging to the Bristol Brigade – and there was quite a heavy casualty list, at times. But nobody of that sort bothered to keep any record – they were all doing their job, and they didn't see why they should merit any special treatment.

MR NICHOLAS

I was fourteen and a half at the beginning of the war. I lived in Whitehall. My father was an inspector at the Post Office, and so I decided to work there too. I used to deliver the telegrams, which I found very distressing sometimes. Ordinary telegrams were fine, but when it was someone that was missing, presumed killed, or killed in action, the telegram was blue on the outside and was marked "Government Priority". When I had to deliver one of these telegrams, the director would say, "Nicholas, you know what's in there?" (that's how they used to speak to you in those days). And I'd say, "Yes, sir."

So I'd set off with the telegram on my bike. At that time the Post Office issued you with these very heavy red bikes for delivering telegrams. When I arrived at the person's house, I'd go to the neighbour's house and say, "Excuse me, sorry to trouble you, but are you very well acquainted with the lady next door?" If they said yes, I'd say "Well, I've got some very disturbing news for them in this telegram. Either the husband's a prisoner of war, or he's been killed in action, and I think she may need your assistance."

I did this on every single occasion when I knew it was a Government Priority Telegram. I think it helped a lot. I spent the whole war delivering telegrams and I got a certain amount of satisfaction from being able to help in a small way, by showing that people cared.

MAVIS DANKS

Before I joined the Timber Corps I worked in an office as a clerk and telephonist. I would have been called up anyway at some point because I was eighteen. The Land Army had been established in 1939 at the beginning of the war, but then they realised that the manpower in the forests was just leaving as the men were being called up, so the Ministry of Supply decided that perhaps women could replace the men in the forests. The Timber Corps was inaugurated in March 1942.

The first training camp was in Suffolk and I was amongst the first hundred and twenty to be trained. I'd opted for an open air life, so I enjoyed it and I went on to become the first forewoman in the Timber Corps. We were sent all over the place because where ever there was forest there were Timber Corps girls. I went to Shropshire, Herefordshire, Devon and Cornwall, because once a forest has been felled, you're sent on to the next one to be felled. We felled, we sawed in saw mills, anything a lumberjack did, we did. In those days you felled with an axe and a cross cut saw, where now they use chain saws. We made telegraph poles, railway sleepers, pit props, charcoal,

Mrs. Danks as Lumber Jill.

anything that had wood in it was made by the Timber Corps women, and sometimes older men who were too old for active service. There were also gypsies who weren't in the war, who brought their horses along to help drag the felled trees to the sawing ramps. There were Italian POWs working in the forests, but we weren't allowed any contact with them at all.

There were 30,000 in the Land Army, but only 6000 in the Timber Corps, so there are very few of us left.

(Mavis Danks has published an amusing book about her experiences, written under her maiden name, Mavis Williams. It is called 'Lumber Jill' and is published by Ex Libris Press)

BETTY LEE

I worked in the Wills factory since I was fourteen. I worked from the shipping room, to the packing room, then the machine room. When the men started to go, I was sent to another factory running a machine. One day they called us down and said they couldn't keep us any longer and that we were quite at liberty to go and join what we liked. So I joined the Women's Land Army. I went to Dursley, out to R.A.Lister, an engineering works that was on war work then. There were four of us and we grew fruit and veg for their canteen.

There wasn't a great deal of respect for the Land Army – we were treated as a bit of a joke. I remember they opened a YMCA canteen in Dursley and we thought, 'Oh good, somewhere to meet up', but they wouldn't let us in. It wasn't because we weren't men, it was because we weren't in the forces.

There was a big camp of yanks at Dursley, a medical camp. I didn't go out with any GIs, but we were friendly with them. I heard most of them got killed on that first landing on D-Day, which was very sad. Towards the end of the war there were also Italian POWs. They'd drop them off from the lorry at our recreation ground, where we grew the crops. They weren't prevented from talking to us, but we couldn't understand them anyway!

Queen Mary came to visit the factory and there was a house there called the Towers which was our central base. We used to go out to the recreation field and we had one field (which was their sports field) with all potatoes in it and round the other one we had lettuce, beans, cauliflower and other veg. Queen Mary came to the Towers after she'd gone round the factory and Lister's band was playing and we were stood there on parade. Our boss wouldn't let us wear our uniforms – he said we had to wear our dungarees. You can imagine the four of us trying to do a little curtsy in our dungarees.

After the war, everybody in the Land Army got a certificate from the present Queen Mother, who was and still is the patron of the Women's Land Army, thanking us for

Mrs. Lee (second from the right).

our services. You also had to apply if you wanted to leave the Land Army and they gave you a 'Willing Release' certificate. I left the Land army in 1946 and went back to the Wills factory for a couple of months until I got married. They didn't take married women before the war, so when I went back a week after I got married, I thought I couldn't leave again straight away, so I stayed until I was expecting my first baby.

MRS ROBINSON

I joined up in 1942. I volunteered to go into the ATS, the auxillary territorial service – I forget that people these days people don't know what it all means. I was put in the heavy anti-aircraft battery, on radar. I was seventeen when I volunteered and I was afraid the war was going to end before I could get in. The whole thing seemed exciting. We went round different places in the country, where we were needed.

We went for our first tests down in Somerton. They tested us to see what we were suitable for and asked us what we liked. We had eye-sight tests and tests like those ones they have in fair grounds where you have to guide a narrow hoop round an electric wire as fast as you can without touching the wire. We also had response time tests. Anyway, I did all these tests and they told me I was ideal for radar, so that's what I ended up doing. We were held in quite high esteem being on radar. I think we were considered 'the posh ones' on the camp.

Down in Lowestoft we had a little cabin that we went in. A little square box effort, and in there were the radar sets. There were four of us in there, all girls, and we used to plot the aircraft coming in. The information went from us to the guns. We knew the German planes from ours because all of ours had what they called the IFF signal, which they switched on as soon as they came over the coast, so we knew not to shoot them down.

We shot down our first plane in Lowestoft in 1943. We all turned round and looked at each other and burst into tears. I said, 'that's some mother's son.' We had to get this plane down and then we realised that there were human beings inside it. Although we stopped the plane dropping its bombs over England we still felt, 'Oh dear, there's

Mrs. Robinson

someone in there.' The navy and everybody were so thrilled with us that they sent us up a cask of ale.

Later we had to try to stop the doodlebugs or the divers, as we called them. They were horrible things. They frightened me to death, those did. That was the only time I was ever frightened. They did so much damage. They were going along nicely and then all of a sudden the tail end light would go out and down they came, not necessarily the way they were pointing – they could come down anywhere. We even got used to them in the end.

Some of the camps were very good. Some dreadful. We took them all in our stride. There was one in Norwich where we were under canvas, which means that we were in tents! We had these duckboards to walk about on because it was so muddy. It was all part of the adventure. We all said that we enjoyed ourselves, even though it seems a silly thing to say now. It was the atmosphere with each other. We were all in the same boat, nobody had much money. We shared everything down to the last fag. If anyone was going out they'd have the good pair of stockings. It was a wonderful atmosphere between us all. We had a sense of purpose, I suppose, we knew what we had to do and we were all in it together.

MRS TRAVIS

When I was about 19 or 20 I was called up – given my conscription papers. My boss said, "If you like I can get you transferred to the factory and you won't have to go." Of course we all wanted to do our bit and I said, "Oh no!" So I went to register at the Labour Exchange for National Service. They did give you a choice – you could say if you wanted to go in the army, or the Wrens, or the WAAF. I said I'd like to go into the Air Force. Once my sister knew I had to go she volunteered for the RAFbecause she didn't want to be left out. I went into the RAF because I thought that would suit me. I think I had a boyfriend in the RAF at the time – but I had a lot of boyfriends – we all did in those days.

I got sent for a medical. We did lots of tests and they said at the time that I would be OK to be one of the drivers. I was so foolish I said I didn't want to! I regret it now of course. But any rate, I went for this medical and they said I would be hearing from

Mrs Travis in Morecambe.

them. Eventually I did, and my family were so upset. I don't think my Dad expected that girls would have to go and do their bit for their country. I was sent a travel permit and I had to go to Temple Meads station and from there caught a train to Gloucester. I was very young and inexperienced as I'd never been away from home before.

When I got to Gloucester there were girls from all over England! They took us all to a camp and they literally locked us in, in case we ran home. It was terribly cold as it must have been about November. There were no lights in the toilets or the bathrooms because the bulbs had been pinched. The water was always cold and if you wanted a bath you had wrap your handkerchief round an old penny and put it in the plug-hole! We got kitted out, and then we were put on an early morning train. We landed up at Morecambe – but everything was done in the dark, you see, so we didn't really know where we were going. We felt very apprehensive and we all cried for hours for our mums and Dads. Some of the girls had volunteered, but not very many, and by this time most of us weren't so sure that we wanted to be there.

There were all kinds of different girls. It was fascinating meeting them all – there were girls from all over the place and from all different classes. We all got kitted out the same. I remember I had these woolly knickers. They were awful – they came down to my knees! We had woolly stockings and hard shoes. We also had a brassiere, and a sort of roll-on affair that had hooks and eyes down the sides to hold our stockings up. There were five of us in a room in the boarding house, but the landlady didn't like us because she'd had boys previously, and they'd been less trouble.

We did six weeks of what they called square-bashing in Morecambe, and it rained the whole time. All we did for the six weeks was walk up and down, learning how to march! In between we went to lectures. We were all pretty innocent in those days and they told us all about venereal disease, they even showed horrible pictures of various organs. I don't think it sank in, really, but it was meant to warn us off, I suppose. We also had injections for everything under the sun.

After six weeks we were all split up and posted to various stations. It was my twenty-first birthday and I remember getting up at four o' clock in the morning and being posted to a Royal Air Force station in Wiltshire. I was picked up with another girl in some kind of Royal Air Force vehicle and taken to a lovely big old manor house, where we were to stay. We were always picked up and dropped off in the dark, so I don't know to this day where that manor house was! It was really strange. Most of us got weekend passes and hitched home. I used to stand on my own and hitch a lift – it was perfectly safe and people would always stop and give you a lift. We were quite well fed, but our parents were ever so short of food. If we could, we'd scrounge a bit of marg or something and put it under our packs, because we weren't allowed to take anything out of the camps. They even searched you sometimes. I used to send my chocolate ration to my sister and brother and when I look at it now, it's no wonder my sister got so fat! My mother used to save all our bananas for her, because she thought she wasn't being fed as well as we were when we were small. When I look back on it I suppose it must have been a strain on my parents to feed me when I went home.

We were paid, but very little. I was a bit foolish, because I wasn't very worldly-wise. I was getting about seven shillings a week, and one of my friends told me that if I allowed my mother a certain amount of money a week then she would receive it as a pension if anything happened to me. As it turned out it was all wrong, but I allowed her three and six a week, so I was always really short of money. We had plenty of food though. I remember that when we finished our food we all had to dip our knives, forks and spoons in the same open-air trough of cold water! That was all they got in the way of cleaning. Generally there was very little hygiene on the camp and the result was that half of us came down with what they called trench mouth. It was a horrible kind of gum infection. They used to paint some kind of mauve stuff onto our mouths and throats. I got a touch of it and they had to paint my throat every day!

Whilst I was being treated I met a girl with a similar problem. She worked in the clothes office and she said, What are you doing with these woolly old knickers? You come round and see me and I'll fit you out with the officers' stuff. They had silky knickers. She literally changed all my underclothes. After that I was silky-knickered and was the envy of all the girls. My friend and I kept her little indiscretion pretty quiet. The older men and women, who were more crafty, took no end of things home. There was loads of pinching going on, but most of us were too young and naive to really notice what they were up to.

There were officers from all over the world there, all skilled men on flight training courses. I used to work on air traffic control and we had every kind of plane you can imagine clocking in. I used to take down their times, but besides that I was just a general run-about really. I got friendly with a girl who was a dental nurse, and when she went on leave I used to fill in for her. I liked the work so I asked if I could remuster – that is to say change my trade – from being a clerk to a dental nurse. That's how I met my husband, he was a dental mechanic and we were all sort of thrown together.

Otherwise it probably wouldn't have happened – I had other boyfriends, you see, so I was a bit spoilt for choice! We knew everybody – it was rather exciting for me coming from quiet old Kingswood as I did. We all stuck together.

Yatesbury camp was really like a big town where you knew everyone. The different Wings had big dances in the NAAFI and there's an awful lot that we got up to that I couldn't tell you about. When we talked about it afterwards we realised that we were in our prime. We'd be doing all the sorts of things that I suppose young people do at university. Sometimes the WAAF officer would say to us girls, "We've been invited to a party at the American base and you've all got to go!" I was rather shy of the Americans, because they were a bit fast.

When the war ended we were very happy of course, but we did wonder what our lives would be like. For example, a lot of my friends were pilots and the ones that survived

Mrs Travis at the Army Dental Unit.

knew they'd have to come home to mundane jobs. It was very hard to adjust and I think it was worse for the fellows, who'd had more freedom than us.

MAURICE MITCHELL

The week before war broke out the atmosphere was pretty frantic. Many firms were most concerned because a lot of them had already lost the majority of their young men, reporting or volunteering for what was obviously going to be a war.

There was quite a lot of building going on. Headley Park, Bishopsworth, all around there was being developed from green fields. If I remember rightly, they were on offer for around £300 a piece, with a £5 deposit in those days. The builders were very worried because they were not a reserved occupation . Those who were in reserved occupations had already been advised. They were generally the engineering firms, which had all switched to the war effort – so the building firms were going to lose a lot of their workers.

After the news broke I remember my mother breaking down because she'd lived through the First World War, and my father was part of that. She could see it all happening again. But my own recollection is almost of elation, because it was something definite happening – part of life's great adventure as far as I was concerned. I remember thinking clearly – I hope it goes on long enough for me to get in on the act – not dreaming, of course, that it would...

I was given the task of delivering call-up papers to the Redland, Clifton and Hotwells area, riding around on my old bicycle. Being born and bred in the area, there weren't many places I didn't know. In normal circumstances that would have been done by a motor cyclists because of the hilly terrain, but the motorcyclist couldn't handle the huge sack it took to carry all these papers. In my estimation it was a complete waste of time – of all the papers I had, I would estimate that eighty-five to ninety percent had already gone to report to their various units, because of the exhortations on radio and in the press. There were a lot who had moved, and not notified the change of address, and I was constantly on the phone, trying to find who lived where, resorting to the old Kelly's Directory. Although I say it was a waste of time, it kept us lads going up to 20 hours a day!

I delivered my own brother's call-up papers, and I remember that particularly because I was in a telephone box at the foot of Blackboy Hill, doing one of my many calls back to Head Office. I happened to spy my brother coming along with his girlfriend on his arm, and he was in full kit – spurs, the lot – he was in the RAF – my father's regiment. So I handed him his call-up papers there and then! He wanted to know what the heck I was doing there, and what these papers were! I told him to open up and see. As I say, it was a tremendous waste of time, and I'm sure many thousands of those papers never got to the people they were intended for, but I suppose it was a procedure that had to be gone through at the time.

MRS CONNOCK

If we start at the beginning, we go back to when I was eleven years old. We were a family of eight and our rare treat was a bottle of lemonade once a week on Sundays. I happened to be in the corner shop when I heard Neville Chamberlain announce that we were at war with Germany. We had been issued with gas masks by then and I ran home to find the whole family round the table with their thumbs in their gas masks, thinking that now the war had started, there was going to be gas. In fact we never had to use them throughout the war, but I'll never forget coming back and seeing them there, thinking the war had started so they'd better get their gas masks out. The youngest was a baby so they had a cradle mask for him.

I left school and had a few little jobs and I then went into the munitions factory when I was about fifteen. We were on essential war work, so there was no need to go and join up, but being young and stupid, seven of us decided to do just that. We didn't know what we wanted to do, but two of us decided to go and join the Land Army. Now I'd never even seen a cow, I didn't know one end from the other as we lived right in the middle of a city, so I don't know why I chose the Land Army!

We went to the recruiting office and they gave us a choice either to stay up north or to go down south. I decided to stay up north, so of course they sent me south to Somerset. I thought, 'Where the hell is Somerset?' I'd never even heard of that. They sent me to a little village called Pilton to do a month's training there. I shall never forget it if I live to be a hundred.

We had a twelve hour journey from Newcastle on the train and the farmer was waiting for us at the station in Shepton Mallet with his little Austin Seven. There were about five cases and three girls to cram in. When we got to the hostel the warden had waited up for us and she said, "Oh, the girls from Newcastle. If you look up in the common room they might have left you some cocoa and bread and cheese, but I'm not sure if they haven't eaten it all." When we went and looked, there was nothing, nothing at all. We were starving and shattered and cold. We went to the dormitory and that clinched it when we saw the iron bunks. I thought, "God no, I want to go home."

A contemporary illustration advertising the Women's Land Army.

The next morning the chief milker came and woke us and presented us with a tilley lamp. There was about three or four foot of ice and snow on the yard and he said, "Follow me." I thought, "Oh Christ, no", but we followed him to the cow shed. We were just stuck under a cow and I thought, "How do I do this?" I didn't even know which end to practice. To crown it all, she put her foot in the bucket and I got told off for it. I said, "I didn't tell her to do it." It took me some time to learn to milk; I'd squeeze and get nothing out and I'd think, "Well, I'm never going to fill this bucket." She'd bring her tail round and slap you in the face and I wondered what on earth I'd done and I wanted to go home. However, I was very strictly brought up and I thought I'd made my bed so I'd have to lie in it. I thought I couldn't write home so I'd just have to stick it.

Eventually I went and learnt how to drive through what they called the War Agricultural Committee. It was for farmers who didn't have any implements and they used to hire them off War-Ag. as it was known. Then we'd go round and do the ploughing and everything. I remember one time when I had to drive up into the Mendips with a tractor and a trailer. This was at Shepton Mallet. I had to take the tractor and trailer from Pilton via the big Babycham factory up on the Mendips. When you drive a trailer on the tractor, it rattles and makes a hell of a row. Anyway, when I got back to the depot next morning, My boss said, "Olive, did you go to Mr Godfrey's farm yesterday at Downside on the Mendips?" I said "yeah". "Well I've had an awful lot of complaints", he said. I said, "Why's that Mr Brook?" He said, "There isn't a dustbin left in Kilder Street, you went over the lot like skittles." I didn't hear because of the racket with the load on the trailer, but I'd squashed the lot!

I went on a few farms and travelled round and I got to like it in the end. I met my husband, Ron, when I was in the Land Army. He'd just come back from India, with the RAF. The farmer up the road had several sons that my husband had been friendly with before he went into the RAF. Apparently Nelson Butt, one of his friends, came by and said, "Are you coming down to Pilton tonight? We've got a new batch in." Ron said, "New batch? What the hell's a new batch? Batch of what, cows?" The chap explained it to him saying, "No, Land Girls, they only come in once a month. Let's go down and see what's there." So that's how I met my husband. He came from Shepton Mallet, so I've been down here ever since.

KARIN CROSS

I went to work in the Guildhall, in Broad Street, Bristol in the Education Department in early 1939. At that time the courts were an integral part of the building. Then later when the raids began we got a bit anxious and thought perhaps we ought to move down to the cellars, and we were supposed to take all our work with us. Of course the courts did the same and then it was thought that this wasn't such a good idea as someone could easily get at the witnesses, so they bought a series of partitions, which were just like a series of loose boxes. We had to pass the court on the way in and we were instructed that we must bow to the judge as we went past (even though we had nothing to do with the court). There were all these heads, the judge, the witnesses, the plaintiff etc. which you could just see above the partitions, and we attempted to bow gracefully every time we went past, usually while carrying huge mounds of paperwork right up to under our chins, which of course more often than not then went flying out all over the floor!

I was secretary to the Deputy Education Officer, which meant we had a lot to do with organising the mass evacuations of school children. By that time, we'd been bombed

Council work went on underneath the Bristol streets.

out of the Guildhall and we worked for a time in part of the Art School which I knew well from college days, and then we moved into part of Clifton High School's boarding houses in Cecil Road. To do this evacuation we had to prepare an enormous timetable, which covered huge walls and of course you couldn't do it all in one go, so each person had to do a little bit, which made it a sort of giant patchwork. Then we had to go down to the station to help marshall all these kids onto the trains, check the schools and see them on board with their teachers and gas masks. The plan had been fine but of course that wasn't quite how it worked out. However it did go quite smoothly as it happened. I think the chaos was at the other end when there weren't enough places for all the evacuees and people were not always very keen to take them!

My mother was matron of a hostel for boys down at Writhlington, near Radstock and at the time of the infamous Good Friday raids I'd just been down to see her on the bus. The bus got back just as the worst of the raid started and they chucked everybody out at Bath Bridge and went off to the depot. I was officially supposed to be on duty that night in the Clifton Report Centre, so I had to walk from Bath Bridge through the raid, up through the city to Clifton. I very well remember, they had sandbags stacked around lamp posts, and the theory was that you used these to dowse anything that started on fire. An incendiary bomb landed at my feet and I hadn't the remotest idea what to do with it, which nobody did at that time. Fortunately a lorry came past with some soldiers on and one of them jumped off and grabbed a sandbag and chucked it on top.

I was on duty then overnight in what was a message centre connected with ARP. Within a specified district there would be a number of these centres where ARP wardens would phone in reports of where there had been a hit, a fire etc., so that we maintained the overall picture. As it happened, it was on that duty that the Guildhall was hit and so I came straight off there, went to the Chief Education Officer who lived in Coldharbour Road on my way and went straight on down to the Guildhall where we started trying to salvage documents until the stairs became so unsafe we couldn't go on trying to tidy up because they wouldn't let us.

I've been rather incensed recently, as I know a number of other people have, about reports in the evening papers about how there was an awful lot of crime during the blackout and how people were just as scared to go out then as they are now, which is absolute nonsense. We walked all over the town in the blackout in all sorts of places. Normally I used to come home across the Downs and nobody batted an eyelid and I never had the smallest qualm about it, nor had any reason to.

CHAPTER 2 – WAR WORK

I eventually went into the WRAF after a slight disagreement with the Education Department. They were expecting us to work the most fantastic hours. We'd be down there until one or two in the morning and at that time you didn't get overtime. If you stayed after seven o'clock on authorised work they would pay you 1/6d tea money, and even if we stayed until one o'clock in the morning, they expected only to pay that 1/6d. I said no, I thought we at least ought to get another 1/6d, which was a modest enough claim. They wouldn't do it, so I said I was going to join up. Women didn't have to, you see, we were not called up. So anyway I did join up with the WRAF and told the education department I wouldn't be there after the following Friday. They still didn't believe me. On the Friday I was still being told what to do on the next Monday. I said I wouldn't be there on Monday and eventually it sank in.

This was the sort of thing which rather riled us during the war, talk about sexism. The men, the dear men had an Italian prisoner of war to stoke their boiler which provided all the hot water on their living site. I stoked ours. As a matter of fact, when I became pregnant, I asked if it would be possible to have some relief from this task as I didn't think stoking the boiler was too good for the baby and they said, 'Certainly not'. I said, 'We've got all these Prisoners of War here, couldn't one of them give a hand with it at least?' He said, 'Prisoners are not here to do that sort of thing.' So I said, 'Right, we save little German and Italian babies, but British babies may go overboard.'

In the WRAF I went to a variety of places in Britain, though not abroad unfortunately, as I would have loved to have travelled. In the beginning I was doing mainly admin work, training people but then recruiting petered out after Russia came into the war. Then one day I saw a post advertised for a job with an intriguing name, it was a smoke screen for a very secret job and they didn't want to say what it was, so they gave it the name 'Pattern Maker, Architectural.' It interested me because of the word 'architectural' as I'd really enjoyed architecture at college. It turned out to be a job making scale models from maps, models of enemy terrain, and models of the types of places where the troops would have to land etc. and they had to be very accurate. They expected a very high standard, you were expected to be able to judge the accuracy by 1/64th of an inch by eye. It was done from maps or photographs or anything you could get on the terrain and of course the precise scale had to be worked out. We covered Germany and all over Europe. Some were of the landing sites for the Normandy landings, some for the rocket sites at Peenemunde and replica of the Mohner Dam, especially for Churchill, that one. It was the Dambuster dam and they wanted another model of it. It had been particularly horrific because of the use of the 'bouncing bomb' which we'd developed.

They woke me up at three o'clock in the morning to tell me about my new posting. They said, "Your posting's come through." I said, "You what? Why now?" They said "You've got to come down now." I said, "Don't be ridiculous, what can I do at three o'clock in the morning?" He said to just get ready. I said, "Who is going to take me anywhere at this time of the morning?" Of course you were not supposed to argue. I asked where I was going and he said "Ludgate Circus." I said, "Pardon?" and he said, "Ludgate Circus." I said, "Don't be ridiculous, what are you talking about?" Then for some reason I suddenly made the connection, Ludgate Circus, Lulsgate Bottom, which is Bristol Airport now, and so I ended up there. I met my husband there, and it was quite good fun.

You can only have independent thinking if you've got something to go on and the thing was that you really didn't have very wide sources of information because it was war, and information was really controlled during the war. 'Keep Mum' was very heavily emphasised and it was very important. I did once encounter a POW on the run on a train. I think actually he was not so much a POW, but an agent. He kept trying to strike up conversation, and we were always warned not to disclose anything about where you came from, where you were stationed, what your work was or anything like that, and he kept trying to introduce subjects like this. It went on for a while and then I pretended to go to sleep and at the next large station I got off and reported him. Somebody else then got into the carriage and kept him obviously monitored and then they arrested him. There were thousands of agents around in the war. It was amazing the extent they could try and pump you for information.

Some years after the war, my husband got a headship at a school and we took a school party to Austria. The kids in the street were still doing Nazi salutes and the people were glowering at you as you drove past, but I think the thing that was really moving was going into a little roadside chapel there, which had a large inside porch lined with photographs of German lads who had been killed. It was a kind of intimate war memorial and it really seemed so awful, you know, both sides, praying to the same God, and just such a waste.

ELIZABETH HOPE

Ileft school when I was fourteen and I went from one job to another. When I was about sixteen, just before I went in the army, I worked in this factory sorting out dead soldiers' clothes. This was just outside Gloucester. This lady worked in the factory and I was a driver there, driving small trucks from one area to another. What you call a Lister, a kind of vehicle like they used to have on the train station. The lady was a good deal older than me, but she seemed to take to me and said she had a daughter named Jean who was a bit lonely and who needed a companion. She lived just across the road from the factory. There weren't many houses together there, the population was a bit sparse and so her daughter hadn't any friends around. I went to meet Jean and visited a few times, then as Jean seemed to take to me, the woman asked if I'd like to move in.

While I was there Mrs Platt and her husband, who were both German even though the name doesn't sound it, used to always have their dinner with us and somehow they always seemed to be talking about the aeroplanes and she was always asking me how far the place I'd come from was from the aerodrome, were there trees there, always wanting descriptions of the area round the aerodrome. I was so young and green it never occurred to me to wonder why she asked all these questions, or keep my mouth shut. I suppose they were taking a plan of the area. I feel so bad about it looking back, but this was a war come out of the blue and I didn't know what people know now, and there was no telly and I didn't read a lot.

She also used to always warn us not to play near the upstairs rooms. She was always stood behind the door, looking at me through the crack in the door. Then I complained one night that I'd heard morse code tapping away in the night. She said it was the boy next door, that he was a bit mental and he was playing morse code with his Christmas present in the loft next door. It was only at night that I used to hear this tapping, I used to hear it quite often. The thing that clinched it for me that she might have been a spy, was that in the room next to mine, which was supposed to be their room, though there wasn't a bed in it as far as I remember, there were coats hung on the walls, floor to ceiling all the way round the room. There must have been have a factory's worth stuck in there. I think it was to muffle the sound of the tapping morse code when I look back on it.

When I wanted to leave, she really questioned me to see why and wanted to know if I'd told the next landlady anything about her. She wanted to know who they were and where they lived. When I went, she came with me, taking my case, trying to find out if I'd said anything. She could see I was a bit green or I suppose I might have been dead by now.

When the war ended, apparently her husband committed suicide. I'm sure they were spies looking back on it. It was a well known fact they were German.

CHRIS BEEDELL

Chris Beedel in 1941 when he started work at Waterfall and O'Brien.

In 1941 I was a teenager, coming up to seventeen, and I was living in Devizes. My father thought that since I was interested in chemistry, he'd get me a job as a lab assistant in a firm of analytical chemists called Waterfall and O'Brien who had a first floor lab in Queen's Square in Bristol. He thought it would give me a practical idea of what it was to be a chemist, as I really had none.

I commuted daily from Devizes on the train for the whole of a year. There were two people working there, one called Weeks, who was an amazing old boy. He only had one arm, having lost the other in the First World War and he did everything with only one arm, even quite complicated things like pouring things out, using pipettes and flasks. The other man, called Toogood, was very down to earth and was always teasing me about being interested in classical music. The boss was a man called Howe who was a strict Plymouth brethren, and rather upright – but I didn't see much of him unless things went wrong. I think he was a warden and he came in one day with an incendiary bomb hanging from a string on the handlebars of his bicycle. He had to call in on us for something before he took it to the police station.

The thing I remember a lot about is my lunch hours. The Centre in those days was just a waste of mud and cinders, because it had never been finished, a few cars, but not much would be parked on it, and a long mobile fish bar – well not fish but spam fritters and sandwiches. I used to take lunch there sometimes because I then used to go to a lunch hour concert in the Colston Hall, with a big orchestra almost once a week. This was CEMA, the Council for the Encouragement of Music and Arts, which became the arts council and they had these lunch time concerts. I'd never had the chance to listen to a big orchestra before, so I enjoyed it a lot. Other times I would go for meal in one of the British Restaurants. There was one in Castle Street and there was a huge one in the Council House, which hadn't been finished then, it was half built and had no plaster or anything, just brick walls and a whopping great British Restaurant in the basement. British Restaurants provided nourishing meals for workers at lunchtime. You'd get three courses for about 1/6d: soup and a main meal and a pudding, very good value, unrationed. There were a lot of people working out in the day and this was a way of supplementing their rations, which was a very good idea. The whole business of rationing in those days was extremely efficient and very fair. Then if I felt like a treat, I'd walk up Park Street to the Berkeley, which in those days had a big restaurant on the first floor with a string trio.

The analytical chemist was an amazing place to work and I learnt a lot there. We had some interesting wartime jobs, some of them quite hazardous. One of the most hazardous, which only the boss and Toogood did, was going down to Avonmouth when the tankers turned round. They had to take a special apparatus and sniff the tanks to see if there was any remaining oil or petrol in them. If there was and people started welding, the whole thing might blow up along with everything nearby. It was a very responsible job and they went down on a motorbike at any time of the day or night to do this at Avonmouth, which was still occasionally bombed and strafed. I never graduated to that particular job.

My boss, Mr Howe, was the gas decontamination officer, in case we had a poison gas attack. Being a very conscientious man, he read up all the literature and he couldn't find out how, if you had butter or flour contaminated with mustard gas, you got the mustard gas out to assess how much there was of it. He thought he'd better do some experiments on this, so I was sent up to Canynge Hall, just up by Redland library, and given a small jar of mustard gas, carefully sealed up in a cardboard box and I went on the bus back to Queen's Square with it. He did his experiments and discovered that it was almost impossible to get the gas out once you mixed it up in the butter or other food substance.

Another war job we had was that somebody decided there might be a breakdown in the water supply. Obviously there had been in some areas, so we had to sample all the ponds and lakes and wells within about twenty miles to see whether they were fit for drinking water. We used to be sent out with sterilised bottles, and lower them down the wells and bring them back. There was some kind of lagoon somewhere I remember which we were asked to sample, and the bottle was about a third full of seagull shit, but we still got our sample of water!

Then we did another job which I was very much involved with. A cargo of Wolfram ore came from the Middle East, from Malaysia or Singapore, the last one to come into Bristol. This was very precious because it was a very important element of making strong steel for gun barrels etc. It came in and we had to assay it, which means you take the whole cargo and sample it very carefully and you get down to a very small representative sample of about two pounds out of a hundred tons or so. From that you work out how much ore there is and multiply it up, and that's the value of the cargo. This stuff was delivered in hundredweight sacks to a big warehouse on the Feeder, which had been a big cotton mill. For two months I went there from Temple Meads and we sampled this Wolfram. It was a very long process.

We did a lot of work for a tannery to tell them how much tanning power was left in the bark – the tanning was done with a funny mixture of bark and dog shit. I think the dog shit releases the tannin or something. It's a very old way of doing it. We only tested the bark, fortunately!

The exciting thing we did was with cows' stomachs from Avonmouth, where the farmers had thought their cows were being killed off by the fumes from the smelters. When the cows died they'd send them to us and we'd size up how much cadmium there was in the carcass so they could claim. Eventually Imperial Smelting bought up all the farms because they got fed up with it. There was also a bloke who died of cadmium poisoning and his widow brought his remains in for us to test so she could claim compensation.

The only other wartime job we did had a perk, as it was checking up on dried fruit. Dried apricots and other fruits came in from America and were preserved with sulphur dioxide, so we were given samples of it to check it was all right. We'd get two or three pounds of it, mince it up, test it and I'd get the remains to take home. My mother would say, "I hope it's not been through the same mincer as the cows' stomachs!" It *was* the same mincer actually, but we had to chemically clean it in between.

I finished working at the chemist's about a year later and went to university as a science student, which was a reserved occupation. One of the conditions was that you did a radio course, because they were desperate for people in radar and also you had to be in the training corps, cadet force. I did that for a year or so and got 8% in my radio exam, which shows how seriously I took it! However, I came to the conclusion I didn't really agree with the war and I thought somebody ought to say that wars were, in the end, pretty useless and ought to be avoided. Even though this one might have a good deal of justification, I felt that somebody still needed to say that wars were not a satisfactory way of solving things.

When I was eighteen, I had a friend in Devizes who was a conscientious objector, who had an absolutely stunning blonde girlfriend. I'm not sure if that had anything to do with my decision but I decided to register as a conscientious objector. I could have just stayed on at university and finished my degree, so it was quite a deliberate choice.

When I registered as a conscientious objector, my reserved occupation status ended and Wiltshire County Council took away my scholarship. I appeared at a tribunal in North Wales first of all. North Wales was rather a special case because if you were a born again Christian, that was all right, and if you were a Welsh Nationalist, that was all right. You had to say, well I'm quite prepared to fight a war, but not with the bloody English and then you'd get conscientious objector status! So I came up there in between a Christadelphian and a Welsh Nationalist and said my objections, which were a kind of Quakerish view really, and I was turned down. So I appealed and I had an appeal hearing in London. It was a complicated business, which was a vast improvement on the First World War when people were just chucked in a prison or taken out and shot. This was all very dignified. I went for my appeal hearing, which was as it happened just two days after the Arnhem Bridge business, so everyone was a bit worked up and I lost that too. I got offered non-combatant duties, and I refused that. I was prepared to go in the ambulance service or something similar, but not to be compelled by government diktat so to speak. A good deal of my feeling was about conscription and the government taking over the moral decisions of the individual.

I knew that when they eventually let me go, I'd be asked to go for a medical. It was at the point at which you were asked to go for a medical that you had to refuse, because

Chris' older brother in Naval uniform, his mother – who was in the W.R.V.S., and Chris just before he went to prison as a conscientious objector.

if you had a medical, you then went into the armed services and were subject to army discipline. The medical was the point at which you were advised to say No.

So I was waiting around and as it happened I went to a place called Hawkspur Camp, which was for very delinquent boys. I'd read about it and I saw it advertised in the New Statesman, and I went there and waited for things to happen. I was a voluntary worker, working with the boys and I got an honorarium of about 10/- a week. It was an amazing place out in the middle of Essex. The staff lived in a sort of converted chicken house and it was a very pioneering affair. It was radical in its time as the boys all took part in decisions and there was a democratic camp council. It was a great experience and perhaps this was what turned me to psychology, which I've been interested in ever since. It was a very formative time, but of course inevitably during that time I was called up for a medical and went to Ipswich. I refused to have it, was escorted by the policeman to the magistrate's court and eventually I was committed to prison for about two months. I was driven off in a car to Norwich, which was the nearest jail, with another conchie who was a Jehovah's Witness who'd refused to do fire-watching work, which was compulsory at this time. This was in early 1945, because we had doodlebugs by then.

The boys at Hawkspur were very excited that I was actually going to prison, and so I went off, and spent about six weeks in Norwich jail as a first offender. Norwich was quite a liberal kind of prison, with warders actually getting to know the prisoners and so forth. I was in the first offenders' wing, which was a very weird mixture of conscientious objectors, deserters, and sex offenders. There were about forty or fifty of us in our wing. There was one very old boy who had allegedly raped a girl and had visions of the Virgin Mary all the time, and there was another man who ran a chip shop in Suffolk who was in there for having sex with a pig. He insisted he'd been shopped by his rival fish and chip merchant.

It was an amazing education. Because I had been to university, I was known as 'The Prof' and I was asked to settle all kinds of disputes, which I got quite a reputation for. They were terribly impressed that I knew the proper names for sexual parts. I didn't know anything about sex at the time, I was just a clumsy experimenter, but I knew all the terminology and they were very impressed by that, until one day somebody came up and asked me to settle an argument and asked me, "Who won the Derby in 1933 then?" and I said, "I'm afraid I don't know" and that was it.

I learnt a lot from prison, the principal thing being really that prison is a kind of delinquent collusion; because there are many more prisoners than there are warders, the warders always have to interpret the rules with some discretion otherwise they'd be clobbered, but not too much otherwise they'd be clobbered by the governor. That's how it still is, structurally, to this day.

I came out and I was amazed how institutionalised I had become. We were quite short of food, so I sometimes went out to the kitchen to bring food into the wing and I'd be slipped something which I'd hang on the window on a mailbag thread so I could eat it when I wanted to. We sewed mailbags and that wing did the prison laundry, so again there were perks there. Poor old boys who were about seventy or more would come up and beg us to give them a nice soft shirt and offer us a cigarette or half a loaf of bread in return. It was an amazing society.

When I came out, I went back to Hawkspur Camp. I came up before the magistrates again and they said they would fine me half a crown. I refused to pay, but somebody paid it for me. Actually I think it might have been the magistrate! I did get summonsed once again after that but I ignored it that time. At the end of my year at Hawkspur Camp, I went back to university and read psychology instead of chemistry. I heard no more until the spring of 1946, when I was nominated as one of ten students to go to Paris on the first international exchange since the war. I had to get a passport and then I discovered that I hadn't been demobilised from being a conscientious objector. However, I did get permission to go because they had a very British system whereby if you'd been a conscientious objector you were demobilised in terms of age and length of non-service. It's quite logical in a way - the longer you'd been objecting, the older you were and the quicker you got crossed off the list. I'm not sure if they crossed me off the list, but they gave me permission to go and let me have a passport.

I went to Paris, which was interesting as all my contemporaries over there had been in the Resistance. They were very understanding however, and said, "You had your situation and we had ours and we both did what we thought was right."

I've often thought about it since, especially at the end of the war when the discovery of the camps of Belsen and Auschwitz and others was in the news. It was horrific, but it confirmed what I thought in a way. One of the reasons I'd been involved in the first instance was because of the Bishop of Chichester complaining in the House of Lords about carpet bombing, long before Dresden, in about 1943. Then there was Hiroshima, and both these things confirmed my anti-militarism and feeling against conscription. I don't regret it; given my age and what was going on, I think it was quite a proper thing to do.

DR STEPHEN STOKES

I became a medical student at the outbreak of war. I remember being sent along to the university to enrol. And the lady looked at me across the desk – I asked were there any vacancies for medical school? She thumbed through some pages and said, "Yes, certainly! That will be £27.10!" Then she said, "You have taken matric, haven't you?" – not, "have you passed it?" I had, as a matter of fact so I was in... when I compare it to what students have to go through today!

I had been on holiday to the Norfolk Broads with some friends, and got back to London three days before war broke out. Germany had invaded Poland, and we thought, that's it. There was no doubt about it, we had to go to war. When I listened to Chamberlain's broadcast, I remember his words very well: "We are at war." It was a lovely late summer day, and it seemed quite impossible, that one minute you were at peace, and then at 11 o'clock you were at war.... and it was still a beautiful summer's day.

A couple of months later my father came home with a crate of tea. He was a bank manager in Bristol, and one of his customers – a wholesale grocer – had presented him with what became a rarity. It lasted us the whole war. We didn't get a lot else – father felt a bit shifty about it!

By the time Bristol was bombed, I was doing a two-year course of anatomy and physiology. This got interrupted because the anatomy lab suffered a direct hit. Nobody was killed, but the bodies we were dissecting were blown to smithereens! Study was conducted in an atmosphere of broken nights, due to bomb sirens at night, and ARP and fire-watching duties, and hectic days. We would be pulling dead, charred bodies from the rubble of bombed buildings, especially in the slum areas of Bristol. But we got on with it. Its what we had to do. People got accustomed to the fact that one day their neighbours were there, the next day maybe not. And as for the anti-aircraft fire? Well, I never saw any plane being shot down by it. It wasn't until the night squadrons got going, with night-adapted vision, that there was any difference.

I went into the mounted home guard at one point, which was really a Fred Karno's outfit. We were stationed at Moreton Court, where there were some of the best horses around. We cantered around the countryside, into the Mendips, looking for spies and paratroopers landing! All we had were two revolvers and four rounds of ammunition... One day I was out riding with some other friends, and about two to three hundred German bombers came over for a raid on Filton. We got ourselves smartly into a field and watched twelve spitfires take off from Filton, where there was a squadron. This lot came over, and there was a lot of shooting and bombing. A German bomber was shot down, and as it plunged out of the sky I thought, 'this is their last minute on earth.' The others were all cheering and shouting, and I started too. But suddenly I stopped and thought, why? Why have we got all this nonsense every twenty-five years or so? Hell, I'm a medical student, I'm supposed to be saving lives. This is madness.

With finals came the serious stuff, when your days started early in the morning and finished late at night. Penicillin had been in for a few months by the end of the war. It was extremely scarce, and meant four-hourly injections. We also had M&B – the sulphonamides developed from a German product, by Bayer, before the war. It was extremely useful. If wounds were infected, what we did was irrigate them, cut out dead tissue where necessary, and put on antiseptics. It was your antiseptic technique which got wounds healed then, and the infected wounds took a lot longer to heal than they would today under antibiotic cover.

When the Americans came to Bristol, they had a lot to do with the extension of Frenchay Hospital, and that was where the burns unit was. Apart from cleaning wounds, the way we dealt with burns then was with analgesics and morphine. Although there were a surprising amount of drugs available then, there wasn't, of course, the range we have today.

I was doing midwifery at Southmead, and one day I was sent out to Horfield Common, where a gypsy fair had been set out. The woman in question was in a caravan, with bunk beds. She was in labour on the bottom bunk, and the midwife and I had just a strip of carpet as wide as a mat to work on, beside the bunk. If you straightened up, you'd crack your head on the bunk above! Following the successful delivery I was made a gift of a packet of razor blades, which being made of steel were in short supply. It was terribly nice of them, although they were quite the worst razor blades I've ever tried to shave with! But I did appreciate the thought.

Midwifery during the raids had its hilarious moments. I remember very vividly going to a house on Cotham Brow. When I went in there was a raid going on, and the mother, who was having her second or third baby, was sitting on a pot, on the dining room table, with a blanket around her. The midwife was sitting on a chair. I wondered, what do we do here? The woman said, "I always have my babies like this, and I'll tell you when I'm ready to be delivered, which is when I'll get off the table!" So the midwife and I sat down with a mug of tea each, with her bag on a side table, and we had a little tea party while the bombs were raining down outside. She said her husband was overseas, but when he came back he was to go to the vet and get himself seen to, because she wasn't having any more of this..!

There were a lot of babies born when the husband was overseas, and obviously not the father of the child. There was a mixed social reaction to this... it was very difficult if the woman was attractive, got a lot of attention, and was drawn into a situation from which it was difficult to extricate herself. There was understanding, but condemnation also, especially from women who had behaved themselves.

There were a lot of GIs' babies, white and coloured, born as well. There was certainly a great resentment on the part of British soldiers towards the GIs', They could take girls out, give them expensive presents, silk and nylon stockings, pens – all gifts that the average British soldier could not afford.

Relations between differing ranks of Americans were very casual. Just before the end of the war I worked for the ARP again during a holiday. I was mainly driving, taking goods around from one place to another. I was asked to go down to an American camp. The entrance was a hole in the hedge, and there was a negro soldier leaning against the hedge, with his arm around a girl. He was the only sentry around, and said "Yeah, what do ya want?" I said I had a message and a parcel for his C.O. from the Chairman of the District Council, one Sir Seymour Williams. The sentry (whose gun, incidentally, was leaning beside him against the hedge) squeezed his girl a little tighter as he turned around and shouted to an officer about 30 yards away, "Hi, Joe! There's a message for you from a guy named Williams!" That was perhaps an extreme example, but there was a casualness, not the crispness we were used to from the British soldiers.

I was at the receiving end of the racial tensions between black and white GIs at the end of the war. I was a casualty dresser, as the hospital was very short of house physicians, and so students did quite a lot in the way of minor surgery. There was a regular punch-up on Friday night outside the pub at the bottom of St. Michael's Hill near the BRI. This pub was frequented by black GIs. We'd look at our watches and say, "They'll be down any minute!" Then we'd have the American Military Police down, who were tough thugs. They used to lay about them, into black and white soldiers – but one rarely saw an injured white soldier. Once they had a gun battle in Old Market, MPs shooting black GIs, and I remember soldiers coming in with gunshot wounds. It was a bit disconcerting – we just hoped they'd take the same belligerence over to France!

At the end of the war, I did some work as a medical officer in the RAF, and had quite a lot to do in the Displaced Persons camps, and German POW camps. The German camps were absolutely spick and span – as you'd expect. They were very good at making furniture and comforts for themselves out of packing cases and pieces of wood. But one came away from the Polish camps feeling terribly sad, because there was such a miserable atmosphere. There were a lot of academics who had fled the Russians. Goodness knows how they had got to England. They were swimming in the treacle of officialdom and were in transit – one knew not to where. They had nothing. So I found that the emotional aftermath of war could be as harrowing as the physical destruction I'd seen.

MR SHAW

When I was sixteen I worked at Shepton Mallet station, loading and unloading the sixty or seventy trucks of army supplies that came in every day to be transferred to the depot. Outside the prison there was also a timber dump, with wood stacked house-high. American prisoners from the U.S. army jail in Shepton Mallet were always there at the station, working under armed guard. There was also an Italian POW camp at Malmesbury, and prisoners from there would also work at the station, although not under such close supervision. All the other workers at the station were over retirement age, because the young men had gone to war.

There came the day when prisoners from Shepton Mallet jail were being transferred to the coast, because it was the day after D Day. They were going across to be landed on the beaches where they would unload stores and equipment from the boats. We were told to be at work by half past six that day. Living on the opposite side of the town to the station, I followed the route that the prisoners were actually taking. To my amazement, at the crossroads there were cars with machine guns on tripods along the road. At the station approach there was a little bridge going from one platform to another, and there were machine guns set up there as well. Not long afterwards, the first prisoners arrived. As far as I can remember, they were all in one column, handcuffed to each other. They were all American convicts, white and black, their blue uniforms with the white arrows on them, with funny sledge-type hats as well. They had to be on the opposite platform, so they had to cross the bridge, and the machine gun had to be taken down.

When the train arrived, they were all loaded on, the carriage doors were locked, and away they went, in the direction of Bournemouth. But late at night they arrived back again, because the channel had been so rough they couldn't be put on a boat to go across. So they were all returned to the prison for the night. Two days later the whole procedure was repeated and away they went again.

After D Day all the ambulance trains started coming through. They used to stop at Shepton – not to let anybody off, but because the engines that were pulling the coaches were clapped out, and they didn't have enough steam to get up over the Mendips' summit in one go! God knows where the destination for those wounded was, but there used to be twelve coaches full of wounded soldiers stretched out on racks four stretchers high.

We always knew when there was going to be an execution at the prison, because the evening before, the executioner Pierrepoint used to come in on the 5.25pm train from Bath and take a taxi to the local hostelry. Then he'd catch the express the next morning, his duty done...

As the youngest person at the station, I was designated to walk from Shepton to Malmesbury each week to carry two gallons of paraffin from one station to the other, cleaning and replenishing the lamps along the way. It doesn't sound much, one gallon in each hand, but I can assure you that walking up that hill was exhausting! One particular Friday it was pouring with rain, and I was fed up. I got to the viaduct, where there was scaffolding to repair the bridge. To get out of the rain I climbed in underneath the scaffolding, under the arch. There was old Tom Corbin, the mason from Shepton, repointing the cement. We stopped for a chat and a cigarette, when a train thundered past overhead and lumps of cement started falling off. I looked at Tom and said, "My God, is this safe?" He said if it wasn't safe he wouldn't be there! Four hours later half of the bridge collapsed!

MR BLACKER

On Sunday morning 3rd September, 1939, I stood outside the White Hart in Shepton. It was a beautiful morning. The landlady had the window open, and at 11am I heard Chamberlain say that we were at war with Germany. My mother came to the door, crying, because she had lived through the First World War. She said, "Son, you're only fourteen – you won't have to go. It will all be over in six months." Yet I finished up serving from 1942 – 46.

We were all keen to do our bit and even though I was only fourteen, I joined the Shepton Mallet Rescue Party. In November 1940, the siren went at teatime. The sky was alive with the roar of planes heading north, towards Bristol. Shortly afterwards the bombing crescendo started, and it could be heard many miles away. About ten of us went to the garage where we were on duty. We stood in the lane next to the depot and watched the sky become alight with the flames of Bristol. We were twenty miles away, yet we could see the time on our wristwatches in the glow. As the controller of the ARP in Bristol called for help to all rescue parties in the neighbourhood, the telephone went dead in his hand. So we were unable to assist, not knowing where to go, and in Bristol the ARP couldn't understand why nobody had arrived to help.

Then in January 1941, Weston-Super-Mare was attacked. It was a freezing cold morning, about 4.30am. We were called on to assist at Weston, and we left Shepton in the back of an open lorry. We we so cold that at Axbridge we all had to get out and beat life back into our limbs! When we got to Weston, we went to the Bournville Estate, which had suffered heavily the previous evening. From dawn to dusk that day we dug out ten people – nine of them were dead – and a live dog. Apparently a grandfather, his grandson and the little dog had sheltered in the cellar of this house, in a cupboard. They were buried alive. As we dug closer, the old man shouted "don't worry about me, save my little grandson!" Sadly, as we found them, the grandfather was alive on one side, the dog on the other, and the child between them was dead. It was terrible. I was sixteen and it was the first time I'd seen death. For several days, I could eat nothing.

In the centre of Shepton Mallet there was a builders' supply shop, run by the Cooks. I was sent there one Friday morning to get some supplies. When I went into the small market place you could hear the roar of aircraft in the beautiful, clear, cloudless sky. I looked up and counted seventy-four German planes in formation. I had all the time in the world to count them as they disappeared north. That morning, they attacked the aircraft works at Filton. Sadly, many of the workers at Filton had left the works to get into the shelters. Many bombs missed the factory, but the shelters received six direct hits. The carnage was such that the shelters were sealed – I don't know if the remains of the bodies were ever removed. You can still see those shelters today, between the British Aerospace and Rolls-Royce factories. When they put the new road in they bypassed the shelters because they are a permanent memorial to the dead.

We were in desperate straits when France fell, although people were not afraid. Just after Dunkirk one evening I remember seeing soldiers sitting all along the road by the White Hart, drinking pints. They had just got back from Dunkirk and were to be billeted in Shepton. All they had was what they stood up in. They were relieved to be back, but wondering what the future held for them.

Then the Observer Corps was formed across the country, in little huts or dugouts manned by volunteers. Shepton Mallet Observation Post was in a field, next to the railway line. The next post was in Midsomer Norton. As the German aircraft crossed the south coast, one observer post would tell another of the progress of the enemy. One day a particular aircraft crossed over the Shepton Mallet post, so they reported it on to Midsomer Norton. But they never picked it up. So they knew that something had happened to it in the intervening nine miles. But it wasn't discovered until quite a while afterwards, where the plane had landed. An army motorcyclist came around to the little villages saying a German plane had come down – had anyone seen or heard anything? We said no. But just outside Malmesbury is an old Anglo-Saxon fort called Malmesbury Ring, on top of a hill. The plane which probably had something wrong with the altimeter, had skimmed the top of the hill and crashed inside the earthworks of the ring. All four passengers were killed. They were found by a farmer the next morning who had gone out to feed his cattle. Inside the cockpit they found a map, with Liverpool circled in red. That must have been where they were heading. The four German pilots were taken to Wells and buried with full military honours. They were later exhumed and taken to the big German cemetery in Cannock Chase in Staffordshire, where most of the German dead in Britain were buried so that their relatives wold find it easier to locate them.

MR PARKER

I was part of 226 Squadron, flying what the Americans called the B25. They used them to attack Tokyo, flying off aircraft carriers. They were very new for the times, these twin-engined bombers. We were test-flying a brand new one which had just been delivered to the squadron. We went up from the airfield in the direction of Stockbridge and Taunton, and had two members of the ground crew on board, without parachutes – they'd just come along for a laugh. Now there was a procedure which was called "feathering", which meant that the blades of the propeller would be turned 90 degrees so that the engine would stop, and you could fly on one engine to save fuel. You could then "unfeather" the propeller. We followed this procedure with the starboard engine, which went off fine. We then did the same with the port engine, but it wouldn't unfeather. We were flying with one engine, and began to lose height, and saw this airfield coming up at Weston Zoyland, which according to the map was just thirty feet above sea level. The pilot attempted a single engine landing, and after we touched down something went wrong as we crashed into a bank of earth.

Everything went dark and we thought – that was it. But then of course we realised – it wasn't! We were still there! I grabbed the escape hatch and we all jumped out and started slapping each other on the back, while the blood wagon came rushing up. The ambulance men seemed a bit sorry that nobody was hurt – it was probably the most exciting thing that had ever happened in Weston Zoyland during the war! The whole station was in a state of alarm. They rushed us to the medical quarters and insisted we need an examination there and then, bringing us cups of tea laced with rum. But we all passed out A1. We were flown back, and I don't think our C.O. was very pleased to have lost his new bomber. There was an inquiry, but we had managed to keep quiet about our unauthorised passengers, and were none the worse for the adventure.

MRS SWEET

I organised some dancing to entertain people and raise money for the Red Cross. I saw four little girls out in the road, who were just dancing. I said, "Would you like to come in, and I'll teach you some steps?" And they said yes – they were going to do a concert for the Spitfire Fund. So they came in, and although I wasn't a teacher I taught them what my lovely dancing teacher had taught me when I was a little girl. We got to a group of five or six, and did two concerts for the Spitfire fund, one for the Red Cross, one at a school – in Fishponds – when it was pouring with rain. The pianist didn't turn up so I sang in the wings! My little boy, who was three and a half, sang "I've Got Sixpence, Jolly Jolly Sixpence!" But the headmaster was absolutely delighted and gave me a pound, which was a lot of money then. I think I took the girls to the pantomime with it.

Then came the day when I organised the men to dance! My husband was down at Salisbury Rd fire station, and he and six other firemen had volunteered to do this dance. I went down to the station and told them what I wanted. My husband, who knew the steps, did all the rehearsing. I dared them to smile, or tell their wives what they were gong to do! The dance evening started off with these men sitting in a circle, on the stage, dressed in fairy costumes. Their skirts were made out of dyed flour sacks and Christmas tinsel, and the tops were their wives' square scarves wrapped around them. Then they had flowers in their headdresses... They performed a fairy ballet to the music of Mendelssohn's Spring Song. That evening I was sitting in the audience. One of the firemen came to the front of the stage and introduced the dance. They were sitting with their heads bowed, holding hands. Then they stood up – not very gracefully – and began to dance to the music. The audience was absolutely shrieking with laughter, the wives nearly choked themselves, it was so hilarious.

We really let ourselves go during the war, at these concerts. You had to do something. When my husband was on duty, I couldn't live my whole life thinking he was going to be killed. He said to me, "We're all fully trained, and look after each other. I'm going to be ok – you must look after Michael and yourself." So during the raids, we'd sit in the air raid shelter where Michael would be asleep, and I would be writing songs and planning dances for the girls. You didn't think about anything else. I think that was the trouble – you buried fear, although your stomach was in a knot. Powerful concentration helped – you knew you had to get your child out of bed and into the shelter,

The Firemen who formed the ballet and chorus for the 'End of Season' Gala night at the Birchwood Social Club.

and you'd put things in there ready during the afternoon. We all did it. There was one particularly bad raid, and two houses in our road were hit. No-one was killed – they were all in their air raid shelters – but I had come out after hearing the bombs whistling overhead, and I couldn't believe it when I saw my house still standing. My husband was in Redcliffe St when that got bombed. There was a cheese warehouse there, and melted cheese was running down the gutters. When he came back, after many hours, he was given bread and cheese, and he couldn't eat it, though he was starving!

VE Day was absolutely wonderful. We had a street party here. My second son was three weeks old, and he was there, in his pram. Everybody made something to eat or contributed in some way. Our neighbour brought out his piano, and Mrs Finch played. We danced and danced and danced...

KATE GREENAWAY

I started as an apprentice hairdresser when I was fifteen and I'm now nearly eighty-two. I went on through the various stages and I was in partnership with another young woman in a hairdressing shop during the war. It was very difficult for us then because we had three girls working in the shop before it started, then one joined the Land Army, one became a Wren and the other was in the Territorials, so we had to manage on our own.

We used to have to work late and of course the problem was the blackout. We had a half day on Saturday, finishing at one o'clock. I went home to Clifton, which was quite a long way from Kellaway Avenue where the shop was. I was telephoned one night by a warden who had seen a light coming from a radiator in the shop. The radiator was in a back room but there was a tiny little glimmer in the darkness visible in the shop. This was about midnight and he said I must come and turn the radiator off. I said, 'I can't, it's midnight and there's no buses running.' Fortunately there was a lady living upstairs above the shop, so I phoned her and asked her to put the radiator off for me. Despite this I was fined £5, which was a lot of money in those days, yet a man up before me had had a light shining through his skylight, which would have been very obvious from a plane and he was only fined £2. I think the trouble was I looked

Kate Greenaway's impression of the hairdressers 'Eugene electric perm machine'.

too prosperous because I wore a fur coat to go to court, which was probably a big mistake!

We had difficulty getting materials during the war. People brought their own towels and we made up a lot of the things we needed. We made our own shampoo from soft soap, and setting lotion from gum. It's a preparation you get from the chemist and you have to add perfume and spirits and shake it up so it forms a jelly, then you dilute it.

The main problem in the shop was when we did a machine perm. It was called a Eugene Perm after the Frenchman who'd invented it. It was a long and tedious process which took hours. To do a machine perm involved the use of a sort of chandelier coming down from the ceiling and in this were lots of wires with heaters attached. You wound hair on metal curlers spirally from the root down. Over that you wrapped sachets and over that you slid the electrical heaters from the perm machine. The heaters had to stay on for fifteen to twenty minutes. The problem came if there was a raid while anybody was attached to the machine! We had to switch off the machine, take the customer down to the cellar and wait until the raid was over. This was very difficult as you can imagine.

The hairdressers, being on Kellaway Avenue, was on a direct line to Filton. During the blitz there were two terrible raids on the BAC at Filton. I was doing a customer's hair, a perm, and she wanted to look nice for when her husband came home. I think it was her birthday. The raid came and we had to go down to the shelter and it must have been while we were down there that her husband was killed in the raids. Of course we didn't know until the next time she came, but it was very sad. Several of our customers lost their husbands that way.

I used to do an old lady's hair and she was very appreciative. She had long hair, which was quite difficult to do and as she was leaving the shop one day, she pressed something in my hand and said 'Thanks for all the trouble, my dear'. She'd given me a farthing. I think she'd mistaken it for a sixpence but of course I didn't say anything. I sometimes used to do people's hair on a bartering basis. I cut one man's hair and he gave me his cheese ration. I did one lady's hair and in return she made a coat for me out of a blanket. Clothes were rationed and it was a scarlet blanket which made a rather smart coat.

We had a cleaner at the shop called Mrs Dale who was quite a character. She lived in Hotwells in a very tall old house which had an outside lavatory. At night they used chamber pots. One night a raid came, and they thought they could smell gas. (There was a worry that gas might be used in the raids, which is why everybody had been issued with gas masks.) They put their gas masks on and they sat there and waited and waited and waited, and even when the all clear went, they were afraid to take their gas masks off. Eventually they did and Mrs Dale realised she'd put chloride of lime in the chamber pots to clean them, and had forgotten to rinse it off. That's what they could smell and they'd thought they were being gassed.

Another time she told me the sirens went while they were in bed. She shook her husband, who was a sound sleeper and said, "Jerrys are over, Jerrys are over!" He said, "Never mind, we'll mop it up in the morning."

Customers would tell me the most intimate things, I was quite shocked sometimes. I was only fifteen when I started and they used to tell me all about their husbands' conduct in bed and all sorts. Of course it was cubicles in those days so they felt they were in private, not like the open-plan layouts of today.

MR J. BUCKLEY

"Dad's Army" was originally called the "Local Defence Volunteers" (LDV), but was soon known as the "Look, Duck and Vanish" brigade. I joined in may 1940 at the factory where I worked.

We were issued with denim uniforms and armbands bearing the letters LDV. None of the uniforms fitted anyone - we were told this was standard practice for anything to do with the army! They might have been suitable for deformed gorillas or even unusually shaped dwarfs, but certainly not for ordinarily shaped people. As a parade was planned at fairly short notice, the individuals chosen to take part did have their uniforms altered by employees in the Trimming Department. Some of the results caused an outbreak of hysterics...

The initial organisation left a lot to be desired. All the officers were managers in the firm, while the NCO's were lesser lights, such as foremen. Of course, this could not and did not work. Eventually, reason prevailed and the role of commanding officer was given to an ex-army man who proceeded to bring some sort of order into that comic set-up.

The first issue of arms consisted of Canadian Ross .303 rifles, which had been covered in grease since World War 1. Although they were very accurate, with long barrels and wind guages, they had one unfortunate drawback. Instead of the usual bolt action with a half or a quarter turn locking movement, these things had an automatic twist which was not visible. Occasionally after firing and ejecting, the bolt was not always locked and would shoot back with the recoil, smashing the unfortunate user's cheekbone.

For a short period we used SMLE (Short Muzzle Lee Enfield) rifles which were standard issue in the regular army, and finally USA rifles made by Winchester, Remington and Eddystone to a standard design using .300 ammunition. Eventually we also used Browning automatic rifles, Vickers machine guns and MK.36 grenades ("pineapples").

We seemed to spend hours sloping and ordering arms for no sensible reason other than finding a pastime for a bored regular sergeant with no imagination and little patience from a nearby Ordnance factory. Our guard duties consisted of reporting at 7pm to the guard room where we would receive instruction for an hour on various aspects of defence, and the intricacies of the small number of weapons at our disposal. The actual guard duties were divided into three shifts - 8-10pm, 10-12 midnight and 12 - 2am. Then the first guard would take over for a repeat of the two hour spell. This meant that we were on duty two hours on, with four hours off and were allowed to sleep, if possible, on the hard army beds provided. We were also allowed a bottle of beer and sandwiches.

During the latter part of 1940 and early 1941, air-raids were regular and lengthy. I well remember being allotted the so-called "soft number". This was the guarding of the test beds. These buildings were quite a long way from the guard room, and being tall, there was a machine gun post on top of the roof. I was in the gunners and we were somewhat priviledged. We only had to turn out if ordered, so we reported at 8pm and played cards or slept undisturbed all night (air-raids permitting.) As the machine gunners were not allowed to leave their posts it was up to the sentry to fetch beer and sandwiches at about 9pm. The night I was on sentry duty turned out to be the worst and most concentrated air-raid we had had up until then. I went out for sandwiches as required, very reluctantly, at about 8.50pm. There were nosecaps and shrapnel from AA guns buzzing around, and I could hear and see the bombs falling fairly close. I took my time over the journey to the guard room and was advised to wait for a quite period before returning. This quiet period was a long time in coming, and I did not arrive back at my post until about 2am. By this time the gun crew were all in bed and showed little interest in beer and sandwiches, so I tried not to waste them... next morning there was a surly silence and a reluctance to converse.

We had a young man on with us one night who turned out to be a veritable Rip Van Winkle. He had the early shift, so when 8am came he was sound asleep. We tried to wake him, but to no avail. Even when he was rolled onto the floor and the bed fell on top of him there was no response other than a faint sigh. Eventually he was pulled to his feet and dragged around the gurad room, dropped and anointed with cold water. We were given breakfast in the works canteen and we had to lift this fellow on to his bicycle to make the journey; halfway there he ran into his sergeant and fell off... which finally brought him to his senses!

Eventually the air-raids became so damaging that the firm decided to move some of its activities to quieter surroundings in the country, and some of us volunteered to go along. We found ourselves in a village where there was no sign of war other than a very easy-going company of Home Guards. We were duly transferred and took up our duties as responsible members, which meant two of us having to sleep in the HQ (a vacant cottage) about every two weeks. What useful purpose this served I have never found out!

As we were short of cash during this time we also volunteered for fire watching, which brought in a small sum. The full-time Home Gurad also had to do night duty, and the sergeant in charge had been in India as an army signaller responsible for communication between units. As we had nothing better to do he suggested that he would teach us Morse Code if we like the idea. The Works Nurse on the premises had also done some signalling as a girl guide, so she joined in on evenings when she was required to to stay on after normal hours.

After some time we began to get the hang of things, and could send or receive instructions at several words a minute using a home-made buzzer. We also had instruction with flags. With nothing to interfere and a lot of encouragement from the sergeant I eventually reached the amazing speed of 15 words per minute. This was sufficient to satisfy the official Army requirements, so I became a signaller.

During this period of slackness and respite from uncomfortable and often dangerous living conditions, hardly any drill took place. We had a few trips to the local rifle range, and some half-hearted manoevres to test our capabilities as defenders of England, but nothing serious. On one occasion we were all mustered and marched off to a disused quarry where the Commanding Officer produced a Thomson sub-machine gun. Most of us had never seen one except in American gangster films, so we were intrigued and delighted when he announced that we could all fire 10 rounds each with it. The target was a cocoa tin placed on a boulder about 25 yards away. No-one managed to hit the thing once, and the 10 rounds were gone in less than a second! They all went above the target.

I endured the antics of the Works Home Guard until I heard that I would be welcome as a signaller in a company at a colliery near my home, so I applied for a transfer. This took many months, but eventually I was permitted to join the company as a signaller (official.) I found that their standard of signalling was quite rudimentary, and only the sergeant could send and receive at more than ten words per minute, so I became a corporal in a relatively short time.

One of my duties was to instruct several members in the gentle art of "Flag Wagging" during summer evenings. As we were all fond of drinking and resistant to work, we used to move further and further away from HQ, and nearer and nearer to a country pub, eventually hiding the flags under a hedge and continuing the training in the pub...

We progressed very slowly in our studies until the proficiency certificates were introduced and we were required to take the army examination. We had used portable radio sets twice before on exercises. On the second occasion we had only just "netted" (tuned to the right frequency or wavelength) when the order came to cancel the use of radio. But when we reported to the examination room at battalion HQ, we found that all the written questions were about the use and technical detail of radio. Another example of army planning... we did the tests and two of us passed out of eight. It is a great mercy that Hitler decided not to invade this country as I'm sure that a great number f innocent individuals would have been sacrificed unnecessarily due to confusion, lack of experience or proper training, to say nothing of incompetent leadership.

But gradually things improved on the home front, and D Day came. It was quite obvious that the Home Guard would no longer be needed. To some this was disappointing, as a lot of part-time soldiers had enjoyed the nights out away from home, and the games of darts and liquid refreshments afterwards. When the order came for us to stand down we decided to organise a farewell dinner and concert. We had quite a substantial sum of money which had accrued due to many people not drawing their subsistance allowances, and letting this be paid into a kitty instead. This sum was presented in the form of a large cheque to the local hospital.

Eventually we were told that the Home Guard was officially disbanded. We kept our uniforms - at least the boots were useful for gardening! We were also told that defence medals could be claimed when they were ready. I never bothered and I don't know of anyone who did. To this day I've never even seen one.

CHAPTER 3
LOVE & MARRIAGE

MRS HEINSDORF

Prisoners of War had patches sewn on their clothes, to let people know that they were prisoners. My husband-to-be would never go out with them on. He would take them off and sew them back on again when he had to. He used to earn half a crown a week, doing a milk round, and working on a farm. Now we went out with each other about three months, although I was crazy about this other fellow, to be honest! But every time I went out somebody would come and sweep me along – and it was him.

He had an open car – an Austin 7 – and it was snowing, and he said, "Come on, I know where we can go." So he took me into this building. I didn't know what it was. And as we went in, I could feel we were going down a passage way. He said, "Come on, it's all right, it's all right" – he just wanted a kiss and a cuddle, you know – whatever he thought he was going to get he never got anyway – and we lay down on the hay, and were kissing. Then I could hear this heavy breathing. So I said, "Oh! There's somebody in here!" Perhaps it was another couple. So I said, "There's somebody in the hay!" And he said, "Oh, don't worry about it." But I said, "We've got to go." So as we were going back through this alleyway, he whipped out his lighter and I saw there were cows in there! Rows and rows of eyes looking at us!

I eventually had a weekend with him – eventually it did come to that, just before we got married, actually. And he was showing off to his friends, saying that he'd spent the night with me... I don't know why I didn't finish with him then, because he's been a joker like that ever since! He had my nightdress in his pocket: it was so thin, you could hide it in one hand. Nylon, you see. And his friends were saying, "You'll never get anywhere with her," and he said – "Oh didn't I?" And threw it up into the air for all to see!

MRS NEWBY

Getting married in wartime was a rush job! My fiancé was abroad, in Canada, and we didn't know whether he'd come home, or be directed somewhere else straight from Canada when he'd finished his training. Before he left he told me that if he was coming home, he'd bring my wedding ring. Everything was censored in those days, so he couldn't tell me directly what his movements were. But a message came on an aerogramme, saying he'd bought my wedding ring. So I knew he was coming home, but when, or where, I had no idea.

My husband came home to Yorkshire first from Canada. And somehow or other – because we didn't have a phone – he let me know that he was staying at home for a few days first. My mother-in-law didn't really want us to get married. She had three sons and she didn't want to lose any of them. When she heard that he was going to get married after his holiday with her, his mother collapsed! He swallowed her act, at the time. Because we couldn't get transport, nobody had a car, and to get from Temple Meads station to the other side of Victoria Park would have been a problem. So he knew this lady down the road who had an old-fashioned Bath chair, with a wicker front and an iron steering rod, and he asked her if he could borrow it. He went to the station to meet them, and when she saw it she made a quick recovery and walked all the way to Victoria Park! She still feigned illness lots of times, to the end of her days... but in the end it was poor grandpa who went first!

Then there was the problem of the wedding, and guests. Forty was the limit, so you had to offend somebody, as you do at most weddings! We went to Caroline's Restaurant in Gloucester Rd, and they put on a wonderful reception for those days. It was a June wedding and we were able to have strawberries and mock cream. The wedding cake was a sponge cake, with a cardboard top covered with some decorations, because you couldn't get the sugar. But we did have a fruit cake as well, which was a very great surprise, because a friend of ours was in the merchant navy, and had come home with some fruit.

The following November we had the first serious blitz. It was terrifying. I defy anyone to say otherwise. We lost all heat, light and water supplies through the raids. We cowered under the stairs while incendiaries rained down, with the planes trying to hit the goods yard of Temple Meads Station. Victoria Park was illuminated by them. When the raid was over, you wondered how much of your house and street was still standing. One house in our street was ablaze, and the firemen came and put their hoses down the chimney. But it turned out to be the chimney of the house next door! We lost all our windows. The house faced north east, so the wind blew right inside. You can imagine the cold. The emergency repair people came along and tapped some black material up instead, because you couldn't have any light showing. Other preparations for war were quite comical. There was a house with a flat roof in our street, and they put a Lewis gun up there, in case we were invaded!

When the centre of the city went up on that first raid, the railway horses were stabled at the end of Redcliffe St. A lot of them were killed, and their carcasses left to rot, because nobody could get to them. But some railway staff managed to get out those that were alive, and directed them into Victoria Park. They used to gallop around with fear in the park.

Mr & Mrs Newby, with old Mrs Newby – minus her bath chair – on the left of the picture.

Food, apart from the basics, was very difficult to come by, and we were brought up to eat everything during the war. One day my sister and I came home, and there was a note to say there was some liver in the fridge. That was a real treat. So we got out what we thought was the liver, and cooked it. It was a bit coarse and gooey, we thought. We found out afterwards it was melts for the cat!

Then my mother had suffered some concussion of the spine in the first blitz, so she was advised by the doctor to get out of Bristol for a rest. So she went to some cousins in north Devon, in a little village, and she was away for quite a while. In the meantime, my father, sister and I were at home. We all had to work, including my father, so we couldn't go standing in queues for food. Now the meat allocation in those days was two shillings and sixpence per person per week. It must have mounted up, because some time later the butcher said to me, "When are you going to have your goose?" We knew nothing about a goose, but apparently the butcher had offered my father a goose for Christmas. Father had said nothing about it, and had asked the butcher to keep it in his fridge until my mother came home. Well, there were so many powercuts during the blitz that after a while I think the goose nearly walked out of that fridge, so he wanted to get rid of it! But my father was brought up never to waste anything, and brought the goose home. It nearly walked out of the door again, it was so rotten. But he insisted we cooked it. The stench was awful! The landlord, who was a pharmacist, came along and said there was no way we could eat it, we'd all have food poisoning. So the poor old goose had to be buried. It was a terrible shame, and nearly broke my father's heart! He lived until he was 96, and had always eaten the green bits of cheese first, by which time the rest of the cheese had turned green as well... but it did him no harm.

MR AND MRS HUNT

Mr Hunt: I couldn't get any time off for our wedding. I was working on the Saturday right up until 12 noon, and I was getting married at half past two...

Mrs Hunt: Mum was helping me, and different people, but it was one mad rush because he was never there. But he did get the booze in!

Mr Hunt: It was the first blackout that night. When the guests came out, they'd all had a good time and everything was pitch black. Nothing was running: it was midnight, and nobody had a torch. How they all got home to all parts of Bristol, Lord only knows! One fellow walked into a plate glass window! But next morning we didn't get up very early. We got to the bottom of the stairs and heard on the radio that we were now at war with Germany.

Mrs Hunt: I said, "Oh, you'll have to go away." But he said "No, I won't have to go at all." But I was shattered.

Mr Hunt: We couldn't afford a honeymoon. I was only earning £2.10 shillings a week then. I had two days off and was back to work on the Wednesday.

Mrs Hunt: But war or no war, I'd definitely get married to him again. Yes, definitely.

Mr Hunt: We've had a good marriage.

MRS AYERS

I had been married eight years when the war started; I had a son who was two years old. The weekend war broke out there was panic everywhere. My husband took me and the baby to Ireland, to stay with my aunt. I went to mass that Sunday, and when I got back, my aunt was standing at the garden gate, crying. War had been declared – she'd heard it on the radio. A few days later I had a letter from my husband, telling me that as he was a teacher, he was in a reserved occupation, and he wouldn't be called up for at least two years. So I said I was going home.

The following Saturday I took a bus, with the baby, to Dublin. There was to be a boat that night, so we spent most of the day on the beach. Everybody was frightened – the boat was already blacked out and in darkness. It took ages to cross the Irish Sea to Holyhead, because the boat had to zigzag in case there were submarines in the Irish Sea. Then I took the train from Cardiff, and already there were these ghostly trains going past, full of guns, implements of war, and soldiers. Everyone was amazed when I finally stood at the front door in Bristol.

After that there was a lull, and nothing happened until 1940. I was pregnant by then, and because I'd had such a difficult time with my first son, it was arranged that I'd have a caesarean section on 25th November. On 24th November, however, we had our first air raid. My husband had taken our son to his first birthday party in Park St, which was to end at six o'clock. He didn't come home, so I walked up the road to meet the bus. On the way I met my brother, who said I shouldn't be out, as there was something very odd happening. "Look up in the sky", he said – and I did. What I saw in the blackness was so beautiful: fairy lights, like parachutes with a light beneath. I went home, and within an hour or so the noise started – the planes coming over, with bombs dropping. But we didn't know if they were bombs or guns. My sister came home through the shrapnel with a saucepan on her head – we had no protection of any sort. My brother came home well after midnight. When you went to the door, it was rather like hell, with flames and terrible noise everywhere. I was told that a bomb had dropped in Park St. right in front of the Acquascutum shop where my son had gone for his birthday party in the flat above. When the children came out the policemen wouldn't let them move, because all the water mains had been hit and the street was like a river. At the top of the street there was a bus in a huge hole. But by devious ways they eventually got home. My husband was very shaken, but my little three year old boy wasn't frightened. He said, "Its all black and brown and red outside!"

The next day I went into hospital as scheduled, but there was no water to spare in the city. Fires were burning everywhere, and the mains were burst. I was in a top room at the maternity hospital and could look out at fires burning everywhere. I couldn't understand it – we had a river full of water in Bristol!

This went on day after day. Every morning when I woke up, my first question was, "Has the water come on yet?" The answer was no. By Saturday, the surgeon said he would operate nevertheless, with whatever water there was. A lot of nurses came into the operating theatre as well, because he was the main specialist in Bristol, and everyone wanted to see him perform. I had a beautiful baby girl. There had been no marks of strain on her, and she was wonderfully rosy. I didn't see her for about three days after that, because in those days they wanted to avoid extra strain on the babies, and I think they were kept in the basement for safety during the air raids. It was rather upsetting.

The following Sunday there was another raid. The matron, who was a real martinet and about six foot tall, organised all the other patients to walk down the stairs carrying their pillow and a blanket. But I couldn't walk after the operation, so I lay there, getting rather irate as I watched them go by.

Then the bombing started. It seemed to be quite heavy, partly because we were on the top of the hill, and although the bombs were directed at the city, the planes seemed to come over very close. One terrific blast blew all the windows in. There was a nurse left with me, and she was as frightened as I was, poor little thing. The matron came in every now and again and said "Everything all right?" At last I said, "If you don't get us out of here I'm going to walk down!" Presently some ambulance men arrived and put me on a stretcher. But all the lights had gone out, the lift wasn't working, and so they had to carry me down several flights of stairs by the light of storm lanterns. I was laid on a mattress in a room full of other new mothers and nurses. When we heard the whine of a bomb coming down, the nurses would say, "Put your pillows on your heads, girls!" A nurse stayed with me holding a pillow over my head until we heard the crash of the bomb. The noise was so terrific we didn't know what was hit. Somebody said that an ambulance had arrived with a patient, and while she was being carried inside the empty ambulance exploded under a bomb.

Then somebody said, "What about the babies?" A door to an underground shelter was opened, and we heard all the babies crying, so we were happy about that, because they were alive! The staff had learned to move patients so quickly and carefully under those conditions, that I didn't suffer any ill effects at all. The next morning the surgeon who had performed the operation came to examine my progress, and said he wouldn't have believed it was possible to move a patient successfully after such an operation if he hadn't seen it with his own eyes.

MRS BOYD

My aunt kept the Pilgrim pub in Brislington village and all the Americans used to come there. They used to swap their parachutes for whisky and at that time my son was a baby. All his smocks, knickers, pillow cases and everything were made out of parachute silk bartered from the Yanks. I've still got white parachute silk pocket handkerchiefs.

I joined the fire service and I was married at eighteen. This was in 1941. My husband came home from convoying to Russia on the Sunday, we were married on the

Monday, and he went back convoying to Russia on the Wednesday. We'd spent the honeymoon in Jean Road where my sister-in-law lived, and we spent the nights in the air raid shelter, even our wedding night, with all the rest of the family.

My sister, who was an apprentice seamstress, went into the camouflage factory in the town, which used to be the old electricity station. I joined the fire service. I worked at Hemplo House, the fire station in Brislington, on plotting on the switchboard for a while.

In those days you had to put all your unwanted left-overs into a pig bin, so the firemen thought it would be a good idea to buy two pigs. We all put so much in to fatten these poor old things up for Christmas, and kept them in the grounds at the top of the garden at the back of the fire station. The men had made the sty in their spare time. We had to surrender a proportion of the meat to the food ministry, and then we were allowed to keep a bit for ourselves. So come Christmas, they were put down and we all had a joint of pork for Christmas!

We used to have some fun at the old church hall in Brislington when the yanks were in the village. Then during the air raids, the hall was turned into a mortuary, because they had several bombs dropped down there. Brislington was quite badly bombed.

We always went to church with the family. The vicar said that as all the Yanks were in the village, it would be nice if families could invite them for Christmas dinner. So my sister and I kept on and on at my Dad to see if we could invite some Yanks for Christmas and he kept on saying no until eventually he agreed. So we arranged to meet them at eight o'clock to go to communion and then take them back home for breakfast and Christmas dinner. Anyway, when we got into the village, it was so dark, because of the blackout, and there were so many Yanks waiting to be taken home for a meal that my sister and I couldn't recognise the chaps we were supposed to pick up. That was the most miserable Christmas we ever had!

RUTH HASKINS

It was 1942 when we were bombed out of Bath and my husband was stationed at Easton-in-Gordano. He worked on the barrage balloons that were facing Avonmouth docks. He went through all those big blitzes when the Germans were trying to get the docks. We'd lost our home, all our wedding presents and our furniture, and I was pregnant. From the rooms I had in Easton-in-Gordano, the nearest hospital for me to go to to have my baby was the Bristol Maternity Hospital. They decided to take me in early because of my unpleasant experiences in the blitz in Bath, and they were going to induce the baby. I went in on the Sunday in September and had my daughter the next day.

I was in the hospital for two weeks and every time there was an air raid warning, they had people coming in and putting you on a stretcher on your bed. The babies were always put in the basement after their six o'clock feed as there was a basement nursery down underneath the hospital. Then as soon as there was a red alert, which meant the planes were actually heading for Bristol and would be overhead very shortly, more people would come in, just local neighbours and people, and take all those mothers downstairs on their stretchers. They slotted every mother into this basement shelter, arranging every mother above her baby. You had to have a tag on your wrist and the baby had a corresponding tag on its wrist and you were attached to the baby. This was so that if there was a direct hit and everyone was killed, they'd know which baby went with which mother.

It was really quite an experience, and it happened at least twice while I was in there. It was wonderful how everybody cooperated. There were lots of kind people who lived in the little houses going up St. Michaels Hill, young men who'd come in if there was an emergency. It was marvellous how quickly they emptied the ward. This was the big house which is now the boiler house at the back of the current hospital. The wards only had about four women in each room and my room was right at the top of the house, so it got quite lively once the guns started firing. They didn't go to all the trouble of taking everybody down to the basement until it got too dangerous. The first alarms might go as the planes were spotted coming in this direction, but sometimes they headed off to Coventry or elsewhere in the Midlands or the North and so the all - clear would go and we didn't have to move. Of course we had very, very dim lighting. The blackouts were always up and as soon as the sirens went they put the main lights out and very low lights on, with blue light bulbs. When they put you down in the basement, it was even less lit, but you weren't left alone; there were always people there with you, probably one or two men and some nurses. It was just for safety, if the worst came to the worst.

When I came out of hospital and went back to Easton-in-Gordano, I had to have another baby's gas mask. Christopher, my son, was only one year and eight months old and you were supposed to keep to a cradle mask until they were two. In order to get a new gas mask for the baby, I had to travel to Long Ashton. This meant I had to catch an hourly bus from Easton-in-Gordano into Bristol and then get another bus, also hourly, out to Long Ashton. I had to go when the baby was only about three weeks. I travelled on the buses and got myself to Long Ashton to the local authority offices for the area. I wanted to persuade them to give me a Mickey Mouse mask for my toddler, which he wasn't supposed to have until he was two, because there was no way that I could cope with two babies in cradles.

The cradle gas masks were made of canvas and perspex with a rigid frame which covered it, and you put the baby right inside the cradle and strapped the baby down by its legs. Then the only way it could get air was with a little pump on the side, like a little concertina: you slipped your hand in a loop and you had to equally push in and out to get the air into the baby. There was no way I could do that with the two children. So anyway, I got to the office and they flatly refused to change it. I said, "I'm sorry, but I'm not going away until you do." They said they were very sorry but there was no way they could do this, they'd be breaking the law. I said, "That's all right. It's taken me two hours to get here, and I shall sit here." The young lady said, "Well, I've spoken to the manager and he said you can't stay, we shut at four o'clock." I said, "That's perfectly all right with me, I'll just sit here until you remove me." Eventually he came out and said, "Okay, but you'll have to sign this piece of paper to say that if your child dies, it's your responsibility." I said it would be my responsibility whatever sort of a mask I had and so it was all right by me. That was the end of it, but it took me hours and hours and hours to get there and get back again, taking the baby, the toddler, Christopher's baby gas mask which was in a box and my own gas mask. It was quite incredible what people expected you to do.

When we were bombed out of our home in Bath, my husband was given twenty four hours leave from the RAF to help me. In the end there was no one who could put us up and so he and I queued up on the second night after the Bath blitz for hours for a bus and got ourselves down to Easton-in-Gordano to his camp. His officer was very good and literally forced the gardener's wife to take me in. He said they'd requisition the cottage and so she had no choice. So my first home down there was in this grotty little cottage with a woman who hated having me and was most unhelpful. She made rules for me as to when I could go in the kitchen, and I could only go in the kitchen and cook once in the day for an hour. The rest of the time I had to use this great big old fashioned grate in her front room. I boiled kettles up on that and of course there wasn't much coal about. I had to get up in the morning, when I was heavily pregnant , and light a fire to boil a kettle before I could even have a cup of tea, and these big old fashioned grates were not the easiest things to light fires in.

This woman did everything she could to make it uncomfortable for me, so in the end I advertised in the Western Daily Press for over a week and eventually a retired vicar's wife was very kind and said if I'd like to, I could have her dining room and one of her bedrooms. I was there about another twelve months. I shared a kitchen with her, but she was a lady who travelled quite a bit as she had no ties. We got on very well, and then after the twelve months she got very ill, so we managed to get a furnished house the other side of the village for about six months.

In the summer of 1943 my husband was being posted and we decided to be terribly rash and buy a house in Bath. His mother and father were homeless as well and they were living with his brother and his wife. My mother-in-law was most unhappy there, so we bought a house in Wells Way in Bath and all moved in in July 1943. Altogether I was only away from Bath for fifteen months, but it was a very long fifteen months.

Our son lives in Germany now, and my grandchildren are growing up there. I'm a mayor's guide now and we did walks two years ago, which was the fiftieth anniversary of the bombing of Bath, taking parties round to talk about it. There was quite a bit of controversy about it at the time and I did wonder if it was a good thing to do it as it stirred up some terrible memories for me. Anyway, my son and his wife and children were staying in Bath on their annual holiday and turned up for one of these walks without telling me they were coming. I thought it was a strange irony in a way, like history going right round in a circle.

MRS ROBINSON

Mr & Mrs Robinson.

Before the war I lived in a very small village and my father didn't like me going out. We had one weekly dance and that was it. Even then you didn't really meet anyone new. After I joined the ATS all of a sudden I was in camp and there were hundreds of men! People all the same age and no parents there to discipline us. We used to have lots of wonderful camp dances. I remember them playing *Good Night Sweetheart* at the end of every dance. It was just a wind-up gramophone, and for most of the war we just had to go in our uniform, but we had a lovely time.

In 1943 I met my husband in Lowestoft, where he was stationed with the navy. We met on a blind date. There were so many young people on the camp, it was all ever so sociable. My friend had gone into town one day and met some of these sailors, and one of them invited her out. She said, 'Oh I've got this friend and we always go out together.' He said he'd bring a friend along too. She warned him that I was very fussy and that I might not like him; so they fixed up that he was going to sit in the pub opposite our camp and all I had to do was look in the door to see if I approved.

I thought, 'He looks all right!' And that was it. He was on a course there to become a petty officer. He passed his course and we were there for a few weeks together. Then we went our various separate ways but still kept in touch.

At the beginning of 1945 my husband, Gordon, he came back to Lowestoft. He came up to camp one day and said he was being sent his embarkation papers to go to Singapore. Could he get marriage leave to go home and get married? Well that's what we did, I got fourteen days marriage leave and we went back to our village. We were married on April the fourteenth and we were back on the camp by the twenty-eighth!

We had been corresponding with each other for a year and a half and we always said we'd get married after the war. When he got his embarkation papers we thought we'd better get on with it in case he didn't come home.

It was the evening of the 7th of May, and we were playing table tennis down at the camp canteen as usual, when the radio said the war was over. The next day would be VE day and everybody would have a public holiday. So we celebrated VE day together and then off he went. That was a wonderful day. The atmosphere was fantastic. He came up to camp for me, because although we were married, we couldn't sleep together – he had his billets and I had mine. Anyway, he came up to camp that day and we got ready and went down into the town.

There were all sorts of things going on – bands playing and people all dancing in the streets. The civilians and the sailors and the ATS and the soldiers. All hugging each other and kissing each other. A lot of people don't believe that my husband and I were together because I don't suppose that there were many husbands and wives that were together that day.

Anyway, we went back to my camp for lunch and somebody had sent up this barrel of ale, so we all had a drop. Then we went down to town again and the streets were laid out for the kids to have some eats. I don't know where all the food came from, because food was short then. There was more dancing in the streets and hugging and kissing one another. It was an incredible atmosphere. The ships in the harbour were all sounding their hooters. As it got dark they built big bonfires on the street corners and we danced round them. We had a wonderful day.

MRS RALPH

I lived on Stapleton Row at the beginning of the war, I must have been about ten at the time. We were a close family and my cousin, who was about eighteen, lived next door. She will always stick in my mind.

I remember the terrible bombing in Armoury Square – my cousin and her fiancé got caught in it. They were running home. I remember my mother going to the police station to check up their names. They were reported dead and she had to come home and tell the rest of the family. All they could bury of her and her boyfriend were their hands, clasped together. I was too young to go to the funeral and it wasn't until I was older that I really realised what I had lived through. The war definitely made us more cynical.

Mrs Ralph's cousin with her fiancé – killed together in the Armoury Square bombing.

CHAPTER 4

CHILDREN AT HOME

FRED DAVIS

In some ways it was very traumatic to be a child during the war, although my memories of growing up in Shepton Mallet are not of devastation, bombing raids or carnage. I was a young child in a family of eight, all struggling to survive. Almost overnight every household had become a one-parent family as the fathers left for war. My father had been a Reservist in the First World War, and was one of the first to be called up. I well remember being dragged along by my elder sister to our local corner shop to buy five Woodbines for Dad to take to war with him. We were late, and the train was already standing in the station, which was only a few hundred yards from where we lived. Then the bloody train started chuffing and groaning out of the station, and my sister went bananas! She flopped down in the middle of the rails, crying her eyes out, because Dad had gone to war without his five Woodbines. She slept with those Woodbines under her pillow for a long time afterwards. That was my first experience of what war was all about, and I was in my early teens before we saw Dad again. And it must have been the experience of hundreds and thousands of children all over the country.

My mother was on fire-watching duties, just like everybody else, and working in the local parachute factory. So the head of the family was the eldest boy, and my two elder sisters acted as mother. As a result I built up a closer relationship with my brother than with my father – because when he finally came back, he was a stranger. I used to look around in wonder at young fellows and wonder why they weren't in uniform – and of course they were in reserved occupations, or conscientious objectors. There was talk around the town about the "conchies", and one or two are still referred to in that way today. One in particular went to lay a wreath on the Cenotaph on the first Remembrance Sunday after the war, and was almost mobbed by the local townsfolk.

Rationing didn't affect the majority of families in rural areas, simply because we'd suffered the effects of short rations for generations through sheer poverty. We supplemented our diets in all sorts of ways. We didn't learn a lot at school – we were out in the fields picking rosehips, catching rabbits and game, or being released from school to work on farms in the summer. All the teachers we had got to know went off to war, and were replaced by young, inexperienced evacuee teachers, usually women, or perhaps one or two men brought back from retirement. When the town was suddenly flooded with evacuees, the classrooms were bursting at the seams, and all the teachers were interested in was containment. Education was secondary. But what else could they do? So we in fact were a lost generation.

We had three evacuees with us in our cottage. There were only two bedrooms, and we were all sleeping top to tail in any case, so they had to sleep top to tail as well. My mother had a pound per evacuee, plus a blanket, but it was decided that the standards of accommodation in our cottage weren't good enough for evacuees, so they were whisked off somewhere else! In fact they are still running businesses in Shepton Mallet today. We felt, initially, that the evacuees were being treated far better than us, although I know there are many traumatic stories about the sufferings of these children. But then I met up with Brian Godden, from London, and we struck up quite a close friendship after fighting each other in the streets. Brian and I were rebellious at school and were caned once or twice a day – not just a "whack of the dap" but one teacher who was as big as an elephant would clout you across the head and lift you off your feet – girls or boys. Brian and I got no education – we'd joke that we had several O levels: O for English, O for history, O for maths...!

Our school backed onto a railway embankment. When the troop trains went past, the soldiers would shower sweets down to us. We'd scramble up the embankment after them, ignoring our teachers, of course, who were standing behind us waving their arms and screaming at us... It did no good at all!

Shepton Mallet was also a reception area for about six thousand Yanks, munitions depots, the Air Ministry, and the prison taken over by the US military. I remember about three hundred prisoners, some in chains and under armed guard, being marched to the prison in 1942. That was their first introduction to Shepton – they wouldn't have forgotten that. It was also my first view of black men – and that was a shocker. I always thought they were twice as high as ordinary white people. But they were nice. If you wandered up and said, "Got any gum, chum?" then two out of three

The grim interior of Shepton Mallet prison.

93

who'd give you some would be the blacks. But I understand there was segregation for blacks and whites in the camps in town. I believe the locals would have accepted them, but the Yanks didn't. There were plenty of scraps. But the Americans went to great lengths to get on with the locals – they'd have Christmas parties for the kids, and give us an orange and a sweet in a brown paper bag. To a great extent I think they succeeded. Some spoke very warmly of them – I know many women did! When they left they said, "We've emptied the pubs and filled the nurseries!"

Many evacuees settled in the area when their homes were bombed in the cities. Their mothers would come down to join them, and then their fathers when they came back from the war. My father didn't come home with the main batch of soldiers. He was listed "Missing, presumed dead". I well remember my mother opening the telegram as she sat at the open fireplace and crying. We didn't know what was wrong with her – and she wouldn't tell us. It turned out that he had been hidden in a barn in northern France. He and an RAF colleague were brought back by a French fisherman, and deposited with the authorities somewhere on the south coast. He was put into one of the military hospitals, and it was some time before they found out who he was, and returned to Shepton. When he eventually turned up, he was a wreck – not knowing his wife, or us, or anyone. He'd been broken on the wheel of violence of two world wars, and rewarded by a pension of sixteen shillings a week.

My mother coped with it because her daughters and eldest son had always helped when she was out working. We had the strength of the family – it was almost like having three mothers in the house. Also families lived in tight communities in the valley, inter-marrying with each other. So we weren't alone – we were spread all down the street, with uncles, aunts and my grandfather. Perhaps the loss of those communities was one of our greatest losses. After the war there was a surge of local authority housing, and some slum clearance orders; and with them the sense of family seemed to have gone too.

I remember our first local authority house: it had a room with a bath in it! What a waste that seemed to us. Noone wanted to use it – it was like having a new car that nobody dares to drive. One of our neighbours kept coal in it. In our street of brand new local authority houses, there were several – ours included – where the tin bath still hung on the back door. We were used to having our baths in front of the open fire, filled with boiling water from the kettle. I was number six in line, and the water was getting a bit scummy by then! So to turn the tap on was amazing, and to press a switch on the wall and have the whole place flooded with light... The cottage had one gas lamp, with no light upstairs. We'd go upstairs to bed carrying a candle, and mother would be up to blow it out as soon as we were in bed.

We also really couldn't understand having a lavatory inside the house. Downstairs was just about acceptable, but ours was upstairs, and that was an awful thing to have to do, if you think about it! We used to have a Dunikins – some people called it a Houses of Parliament – up the garden, and ours had three holes in the seat – one for adults, and two for children, where you'd hide away if mother wanted you to scrub the flagstone floors. To bring your lavatory into the house – it wasn't really on...

Our new neighbours came from a little further down the valley, but they might as well have come from Bristol, or elsewhere. They were foreigners. It was ages before people would speak over the garden fence as they had done.

MRS BUNYAN

I've still got the homework that was never marked – I must have been about fourteen. We got as far as Stokes Croft on the tram and then we had to pick our way through the rubble. When we got to the corner where our school should have been, an air raid warden told us we weren't allowed to go any further. There was no school left. It used to be Bristol Junior Commercial School.

We were without a school for about three months. Strange, we didn't feel overjoyed: actually, I think we were a bit sad. For one thing we had to turn round, pick our way over the rubble again and find our way home. They eventually found us a property in Red Cross Street which had been condemned, but they revitalised it for us. We liked it, but the atmosphere was a bit strict. Air raids were no excuse for not doing your homework! I remember even getting into trouble for not wearing my hat outside school. I think they were a bit over-strict to make sure we continued day to day life as normal.

One night my Dad and my brother and I were coming home from church when there was an air raid, and we had to run up some hill with all these shells going off overhead. What I remember most clearly is getting a stitch. We were in real danger, and I suppose we must have been a bit scared, but all I remember is getting that stitch. We got so used to it all, you see. Everything carried on more or less as usual: it would just be, "Oh hurry up and get your homework done in case we have to get down the shelter!"

I was also in the Women's Junior Air Corps; and on my spare couple of evenings I used to go to the ATC squadron up on Filton Road and help out with the typing. To be honest, I can't really remember what we had to type, but they kept us pretty busy – in the intervals we even served the squadron tea and coffee. I remember Queen Mary, the Queen Mother as she was then, inspecting us on the Downs. Then we all marched down Park Street and into the town. We all felt ever so patriotic! Another thing that used to make me proud was cleaning out the sump from our air raid shelter. It was basic, but it was like my little home.

*Mrs Bunyan (on the right of the picture)
with a friend*

MARJORIE ABBOTT

I remember that fateful Sunday when the Prime Minister, Neville Chamberlain, told a listening nation over the wireless that we were at war. I recall how, expecting immediate violent death and destruction from the skies, the forty children in my junior class suddenly felt like precious, innocent children whom I dearly loved and wanted desperately to protect. This probably wasn't how I generally felt about them of course!

As the war gradually became our way of life, we even found something to laugh about in the midst of all the air raids, bombs and falling shrapnel. The shrapnel, incidentally, was avidly collected by the kids and was probably as important to them as computer games are to children today.

When there had been a bad raid the night before, we deliberately got the children to talk about their grim experiences in school the next day, to help get it out of their sys-

Mrs Abbott's junior class.

tem. One night the terraced house where a girl called Gracie lived was badly damaged by incendiary bombs. The next day she came out to the front of the class to tell us about it and said, nonchalantly, "Well, see, now our Dad's in the army, we all sleeps together downstairs in the front room 'cause of the bombs an' that. Well, see, our Mum and our Shir and our Dave was in bed and the sirens had gone. Our Mum woke up and put out 'er 'and and touched the wall and she said to our Shir, "'ere, isn't this wall gettin' ever 'ot!" and that was 'cause our 'ouse was on fire."

Then there was Billy who was present one morning but failed to turn up in the afternoon. After calling out the register, I asked if anyone knew why he was absent. Someone volunteered the information, "Miss, I seen 'im in the dinner hour, 'e was playin' on 'is Auntie's des-briz." So much for the horror surrounding the newly bombed house of a close relative – to Billy it was a new place to play, attractive enough to justify truancy, or 'mooching' as Bristol children called it.

Alan was perhaps a prime example of taking the horrors for granted. He himself had been buried in the bombed wreckage of his home and had tragically lost his leg in what was then called 'an incident'. He had an artificial leg, but as he was still growing, it had to be changed constantly and it can't have been very comfortable. It was amazing how quickly he'd become quite agile, despite this, and even capable of using his wooden leg to advantage. He used to stick it out in the gangway between the desks in the classroom to trip up his classmates and of course it didn't hurt him at all. The victim would complain, "Yere miss, it ain't fair, Alan's stuck out 'is wooden leg on purpose!" Once Alan was caught stealing a bicycle and though of course I had to tell him off, I couldn't help secretly admiring this one legged thief.

Paper for art lessons in school was virtually unobtainable, so the children had to bring newspapers from home to paint their masterpieces on. One of my colleagues was transferred to a more prosperous area around this time and when we asked how the work of the children compared with that of the children in our school, she said, "Well, the art is rather better, somehow it looks more effective on the pages of the Telegraph than on those of the Daily Mirror!"

When evacuations of the children began, there was a lull in the nightly air raids and some of the evacuees started returning home. Teachers were urged to discourage this and one day I noticed a boy called Kenny was back after a very brief trip to North

"Devon." I said reproachfully, "Kenneth, I thought you were evacuated."

"No Miss,"he said "I come on back." I asked him why and he said "Apple pie for breakfast, apple pie for lunch, apple pie for tea and for supper, apple pie. So I come on back." It seems he could accept the bombs and the sirens, but not a change in his diet!

One day the class were busily writing compositions when one boy, called Raymond, looked up from his laboured writing and announced very seriously, "Miss, d'you know what, you don't 'ave fish now wiv a fourpenny lot, you gets sausage!" This was his observation of the latest kind of war casualty.

However as the war went on, the long nights spent in air raid shelters of one kind or another took their toll. After perhaps fourteen hours spent in the over crowded tunnel of the disused Clifton Rocks Railway or in the reinforced cellars of local factories, the children would turn up late at school looking bleary and grubby and not really fit for lessons. They started getting ringworm, dermatitis and headlice. Yet two of my nine year olds, Stewart and Keith, managed to write a poem, part of which ran:

> We are in a private shelter
> Under a factory so gay,
> It's W.D.& H.O. Wills's,
> So all the people say.
> Ack Ack on the ground,
> Spitfires in the sky,
> Safe in the shelter,
> What care I?

BRYAN HAYNES

I was about seven or eight when war broke out. I remember the change in atmosphere quite distinctly. From the moment my Father told me that we were at war with Germany it somehow immediately brought me to life. From being a very little boy in a bit of a haze, I seemed to listen and look and observe a great deal more than ever before.

One of my clearest memories is when I was playing with some friends in a disused communal air raid shelter in Coronation Road. It was the best playground we ever had – it smelled of wood creosote and clinker, and the old gas curtains just made the place even more appealing to us. The whole area was enclosed in wire mesh and often patrolled by a duty warden, but that didn't stand in our way – if anything it made it more exciting!

On one particular occasion, it was a Saturday I think, the aircraft were flying extremely slowly and very low. We were thrilled by the fact that we could actually see the man in the passenger seat behind the pilot, so we waved up to him. To our great surprise he waved back! We could even see that he had a clipboard in his hand. It was only when we heard the duty warden swearing at us, and then spotted the crosses on the side of the plane, that we realised that we had been waving at the enemy! I think that they were probably flying back from the BAC base and the man in the passenger seat must have been making notes. We kept very quiet about that incident, as waving at the baddies was hardly something to boast about... Later that same day I was shopping down in Castle St. with my parents when there was an air raid. Everyone piled into St. Peter's church because no one thought that churches would be bombed, but within a week it had been hit. Things like that gave you a sense of foreboding.

We heard about most things via word of mouth. I remember hearing about a near miss of our neighbours, who lived three doors up on West Park. She was running to catch a bus one day and the driver can't have seen her, because the Bristol Blue drivers would always stop if they saw you. She missed it, and later on she found out it had been bombed. She was completely shaken by the knowledge of having been so close to getting killed.

Everyone needed bringing out of themselves, and our saving grace was that the new theatre was untouched. It was always chock-a-block because the films only lasted about an hour. People's attitude was, 'if I'm paying a shilling to go and see an hour long show, then at least I haven't missed what I would have missed if I'd gone to see a two and a half hour show in an ordinary cinema.' The Bristolians were a pragmatic bunch even then!

Brian Haynes during the War.

MR HIGGINS

The blitz started for us without any warning at all. There had been raids, up north and in Coventry, but when the Brislington raid started, we just didn't get any warning. The planes came overhead and we just assumed they were ours, we'd been told there were plenty of planes in those days, we didn't realise there weren't any. It wasn't until the bomb was hurtling down on us that we realised what it was. There was a mad rush then, and although we had an Anderson shelter, there was no time. I remember the moment most vividly, the screech of the bomb was like something out of hell, and I had to be dragged inside to the understairs cupboard, because I was almost hypnotised by the noise. No one had any idea really what the thing would be like. There was a big bin under the stairs which held chicken food, because we'd all been encouraged to keep chickens, and my mother held that over her head. I think she felt if she had that on her head, everything would be all right. The bang was absolutely enormous. It literally shattered the house. They were semidetached houses and the back door shot off in one direction down the garden, but the lock on it, which was a big heavy rim lock, shot off, went straight through the wall in the kitchen, straight through into next door and destroyed their very early version of a washing machine. It was an incredibly expensive piece of equipment, no one else had one or even dreamed that these things were about. Once the biggest shock about the bomb had gone, that was what everyone in the street talked about for weeks!

Once the raids had started in earnest, there were lots of interesting things to do. You could explore bombed houses and no one ever stopped you really. Nowadays it wouldn't be allowed because they were in a pretty dangerous condition, but as kids, we had to go to school and everything carried on as normal so we just investigated them. I remember we made lead soldiers as there was tons and tons of water pipe around and we'd light fires with the lathes from the ceilings to melt the lead, make a mould in clay from a pre-war soldier somebody had and make lead soldiers.

On occasion when we went to school, there'd sadly be a new empty place, meaning another bomb victim. The worst time this happened, when there were lots of empty places, was after one of the two giant gas tanks in Brislington had been hit. This was about a week after the kitchen incident and it was obvious that they were determined to target the gas cylinders. The tanks floated on millions of gallons of water. They were bottomless cylinders resting on water, which were pushed up by the gas pressure. The attendant had apparently done his level best to avert a disaster and to some extent he did. He prevented a massive explosion by letting out a lot of the gas, but he lost his life into the bargain when the cylinder was hit. It was obvious they were targeting the gas tanks when they dropped numerous flares all round and I think there were in the region of thirty bombs in the first onslaught. Seven houses in our street went that night and unfortunately when the gas tank went, the cylinder quickly subsided into the water which then spilled into the streets. In Marksbury Road, which was right under the gas tanks, whole families were drowned in their Anderson shelters as the millions of gallons of stinking water flooded them. They didn't stand a chance. There were lots of people missing and at the bottom of our road there was a Mrs Haines who had a very young baby about two months old and another two older children who were trying to escape with her from the water in her house. The baby was lost in the flood and drowned. It was dreadful. As children I think it was these events involving people we knew that brought home the full horror of the war, when your friends were killed or someone really close to home. Of course these tragedies occurred to thousands of people across the country.

Strangely enough, although we didn't have family holidays, we did get a school camp. There was a youth education camp at Brean, just up on the Down. We'd all go to Bedminster station to catch our train, of course it was all steam trains then, and we were all told that we had to tell the guard to stop at Brean Halt. Even in those days nobody knew where it was. I'll always remember that on the bank at Brean Halt Station there were thousands of juicy wild strawberries, which was wonderful because in those days you didn't see much fruit. Then we had to get three miles from the Halt, at a time when there was no transport, and so we had to carry our own bags all the way. It didn't half get heavy after the first mile! The teachers would try to encourage us by saying, 'It's just around the next corner!' and then at the next corner, 'It's just around the next corner!' All the excitement begins to wear off by that stage. When we got there, there were about twenty bell tents, heavily worn by the years, and duck-board floors and so even then, we still had to go down the road to the farmer's loft and fill up our palliasses with straw. That's what we slept on. But with the food and everything, those teachers couldn't have done better. It was idyllic really because you got away from all this terror and bombing. At least we thought we were, but on the first camp, we were hoiked out of bed at midnight one night and sent down into little slit trenches to watch the bombing of Weston-super-Mare. When we watched it, it felt like watching a firework display, because what was happening on the ground didn't seem to affect us, perhaps because of the distance. We watched planes dive through the searchlights, barrage balloons catch fire and crash to the ground. There were some

Bofors guns on the beach at Berrow which were going like hell all the time like 'chatter, chatter, chatter' and occasionally bigger, heavier anti-aircraft guns like Purdown Percy could be heard as well. A lot of the German aircraft, in a fit of bravado, used to dive down in the searchlight beams and try and gun the searchlights out. The actual tragedy of what was going on was lost in our wonder at the spectacle.

Whenever aircraft did come down back in Bristol, there'd be a mad rush to get to the site, not because we were morbidly curious, but because all the kids used to collect the perspex. We used to make rings out of the tiny pieces, taking a threepenny bit (old threepenny bits had many sides), we shaped the perspex round this and then burnt a hole in the middle with a poker big enough for your finger and then you could shine them up by rubbing them on your trousers. We thought they were wonderful.

After the shelters had all been flooded when the gasometer was hit, we usually tried to reach the public shelters in Parson Street School, but sometimes there was insufficient warning and we'd use our Anderson shelter. One night when we were forced to use the Anderson shelter and my father was out fire-watching at Robinson's factory, an air raid warden came and opened the door of the shelter saying, "Out! There's an unexploded bomb in the road opposite."

The journey to the school shelter was breathless and hazardous. My mother had the baby in her arms and my younger brother by the hand, and I went on ahead, pushing my younger sister in a push chair. All hell was let loose round us and in the frenzied run, I felt a burning sensation across my toes. When we got to the shelter, people pointed at my boots as the complete toe cap had been torn off by shrapnel. Fortunately my toes were all right!

We thought we'd be safe in the shelter, but when the school burned down with an incendiary bomb, we had to move on because the inferno would attract further bombs. We negotiated our way through the dark in slippery frost to the brick kilns of the Holychrome Brick Company in Vale Lane. The old kilns were big, cavernous affairs that looked like brick beehives. They were closer to open country, so everyone felt a bit safer there, until suddenly someone spotted a land mine coming down above us, suspended by a parachute. Fortunately it drifted to the clay pit behind the kilns, but the blast was tremendous and sent bricks cascading from the kiln roof. My mother was struck by a falling brick on her nose, but miraculously no one was more seriously injured. Then when dawn finally came and we trooped home, it was only to find that our house had been burned down. My Mum's prized possessions were just thrown randomly in the street and were freezing in pools of water from the fire-hoses. We thought we might save a few things, but everything was impregnated with blobs of tar which had dripped down from the blazing roof-felt. We went to stay at my gran's house in Pensford until we were rehoused.

When Churchill announced the end of the war there was tremendous elation. Bells rang and hooters went like an extra long New Years Eve. It just spread and everyone went about elated for days. A new kind of competition set in then because every street was going to have a better street party than the next street. The competition was fierce!

At first on hearing the news, everyone flocked to the tramway centre in the evening and celebrations went on there well into the night. I was fourteen years old by then and I'd never seen anything like it, it was tremendous. I don't think the anti-climax came until the celebrations had subsided. People then began to look at what was going to happen, politically and so on. There was a void for quite some while immediately after the war. Things were pretty stark because rationing was just as severe, if not more severe than when the war was on. Literally everything was rationed and there were lots of bombed buildings and the desolation seemed to stay for ages. Even sometime afterwards, in 1948 when I was called up for my National Service, it was amazing to me to go to towns which were brilliantly lit and shops with plenty of things in them in Germany. It made me wonder what we'd won the war for!

MR LEGG

I was caught in the first air raid and was buried in the rubble of my house in Lower Maudlin St. The bomb that hit us was the second in a stick of three. The first hit the motor construction works in Bath Road, the second one hit Grove Park Road where we lived and the third hit my school, which was St. Lukes down in the village. I lost my house and my school in one night! That must have been 1940, which would have made me six and a half. No one had bothered about shelters as early as that. I remember hearing the sirens go, then the drone of a plane and I don't remember anything else until my father dug me out. Apparently the door of my room had blown onto my bed, then mother's door had blown on top of it from across the landing, and then the ceiling had collapsed – so I was in a little tent. After my father had got me out we went downstairs, and the silly canary was still singing.

The Legg boys.

Then we had to start wandering from relative to relative. That was the routine in those days, when one lot got sick of you, you just moved on to another lot. Later I was living with an Auntie on Easton Road and I went to All Hallows school. One school day the raiders came over and as we were running from the classroom to the surface shelter in the playground, the rotten devils started machine-gunning us! Nobody was hurt, but when we got in the shelter we could hear the bullets hitting the concrete roof. I think that although we were aware of the danger, it became routine, and you tended just to accept it. We'd go round in the morning, picking up bits of shrapnel, and if they were hot – all the better!

Another thing we did – which was naughty – was to go into bombed houses to see what we could find. We didn't think of it as stealing. I remember that at the bottom of City Road, which was quite posh in those days, we went into a cellar and found a load of glass slides. I don't know what they were for, but there were hundreds of them and we pinched the lot. Another time a lemonade factory off Sussex Place was hit, and we got super collections of bottle labels!

JEAN CROWTHER

I was a schoolgirl in Keynsham during the war. I was eight years old. I remember the moment when war was announced: I was on a swing, the windows were open, it was a hot autumn day. I ran into their kitchen and my mother was crying. It was the first time the gravity of it all hit home.

In Keynsham they had no air raid shelters, that early on. If we lived too far from the school we had to go to someone's house near the school. We had someone who used to help at home, and her mother was going to have us. My sister Lesley and I were sent across the road by our teacher when the siren went. We went running up to Clare's mother – who was out! Nobody had ever thought of this possibility. There was a funny little passage way in Temple St, in Keynsham, and we stood there. It was like watching a film. It was a daylight raid over Filton, and we can remember seeing parachutes coming down. We both stood there, eight and six years old, thinking it was rather exciting!

But on a later raid a bomber came down in Keynsham, and I can remember waking up and seeing this burning plane. I'll never forget that. It was horrifying. The scream of bombs coming down is something horrid – and we were even quite a way away. I don't know how people directly beneath them coped.

We didn't have any evacuees because we were a large family. There were six of us. But I remember Maisie and Millie being billeted on Mrs Jones two doors away. At first we weren't allowed to play with them, because they had nits and impetigo. In those days you put that terrible purple stuff on the poor children – they had purple faces – but once that cleared up we did all play together. They thought we talked funny, and we thought they did! But we didn't have that much time with them, because we went to school in the mornings, and they went in the afternoons. Then after the Phoney War, as it was called, a lot of the evacuees went back to London.

What I can remember that brings tears to my eyes was when D Day started. It had been announced on the 8 o'clock news that we had landed in France. We all walked into assembly at school and we sang *Oh God Our Help In Ages Past*. A lot of the girls were crying, because they had brothers and fathers there. Death hadn't been talked about before, and suddenly it was talked about then.

We all walked an awful lot in those days. We'd go out "wooding", because coal was rationed. I didn't like having to do that. We had an old pram, and I thought it was a great indignity!

At the end of the war I remember my parents going down to the VE night celebrations in Keynsham. But because we had school the next day, they didn't take us, and we were sent to bed. My sister always remembers it, because again it was a hot night, and there were a terrible lot of may-bugs about, and they kept flying in at the window. And I know this sounds ludicrous, being one's memory of the end of the war, but they kept dropping on the bed. I rushed out of the bedroom but wouldn't let my sister come out, and she said – I'll *never* forget VE night!

Rationing lasted a long time after the war. Lesley and I got married in 1954, when things were still rationed. In fact I can remember the night before the twins were born, We ate a steak that we'd saved up for, and a tin of fruit that somebody in America had sent us.

ERIC GADD

I was fourteen and a half – a printer's devil in Bristol – an apprentice. I can remember on the Sunday morning, we went to church. My father was a church warden down at St. Francis church. We got home to Horfield at eleven o'clock and all sat around the wireless, and listened to this declaration of war. What would happen? I was a young man. And do you know, a Blenheim Bomber took off from Filton, and zoomed over the house tops, and I thought, 'he's going to bomb Germany!' But nothing happened.

Now I knew what to do as I'd been collecting cigarette cards as a young boy – W.H. Wills cigarette cards. Now they produced an issue of cigarette cards on what to do in an air raid, how to put out an incendiary bomb – this was all before the war had even started! I always remember How to Stop A Tank – you had to rip up a tram line and jam it between its tracks!

Of course the militia men had started to be called up – the men of eighteen. There were a lot of soldiers about, up at the Horfield barracks. We all had to have these gas masks. I always remember, in the first week of the war, in James Square there was a firm by the name of Roystons. Little did I know it was going to be bombed badly in the next twelve months or so... The manager asked the girls how quickly they could make a gas mask. So he put them through a test, and they turned out – say, twenty in an hour. And so he said, "Right, I'll pay you sixpence each for them – that's what you can earn during the hour." And he put them on his production line, and they turned out about 120 an hour! They made so much money in the first week that poor old Royston was nearly bankrupt!

Aeroplanes were always silver until the war started, then they started camouflaging them in blues and greys. And everything was blacked out. People put frames up to the windows, with black material – everybody made them, and there wasn't a light to be seen anywhere. I remember that we had a light coming under the door, and this air raid warden came around and pointed this out to my father. My father said, "What do you think – they're coming up in bloody submarines?" But they put the lights out on the headlights of the cars – they were just little slits. I remember going up Gloucester Rd. and everything was blacked out. It was quite eerie, especially when the fog came. People walked along like glow worms, with these tiny torches which were blacked out as well – they just had a little circle of light.

Searchlights came in and they were like candles up in the sky – very, very bright. They would reflect off the clouds and light the whole city up. We knew when the air raid was coming because they used to signal with them, going round and round in the sky, signalling to the next light, and that would take it up, and so on, up the country, following the aircraft. But that was much later than just the first week of the war.

I always say that after the war, we should have struck a medal for mums. It was the mums who fed us all during the war on rations. They were wonderful. We never did that – we gave them to everybody who served on the Home Front, but never the mums. But it was a very healthy diet. Have a look at photographs of people after the war – they were very fit and slim. We all put on weight after the war, so that I think this generation is the heaviest that's ever been! We do get lovely food now.

PRUE AND PAM LEE

The photograph of us as dancers was taken in about 1941, when we were ten years old. We went to a dancing school at West Park, and performed every year at the Eisteddfod. We also appeared several times at the Victoria Rooms and at the Princes Theatre, which was finally bombed the night we were due to dance there. There was probably a lot more of that sort of entertainment during the war, and there were dancing schools everywhere. Children of all ages would give dancing displays in the theatres, doing what they could, and everyone would go along to watch. We all went to the cinema a lot, too, and didn't bother to get out even if the air raid siren went. People just got fed up with the interruptions.

My mother made all the costumes. We were blackbirds once, with black hats on, and we popped out of a pie! Then we were "Two of a Kind". We had face masks on the backs of our heads, and came on stage backwards dancing and singing "Oh delightful is the morning and refreshing is the rain.". Then we turned around and showed the audience our faces...

We never knew where we'd be safe in a raid. The first night the sirens went we jumped out of bed, not knowing what to do. We have lived in this house all our lives, and although today we'd be scared to go into our cellar, during the war we thought nothing of it, as children. It's a solid house, but it has a crack in the wall by the door which has been there since the war. A land mine dropped at the top of Hampton Road; probably aimed at the railway lines. I was standing at the door waiting for my mother to come home, and the next thing I knew I was on the kitchen floor! The blast of that bomb had thrown me back fifteen yards.

Prue and Pam Lee aged 10

Our brother was evacuated when he was five to our relations in the north, and we went after that to a landlady in Weston-Super-Mare. The first night we were terribly homesick, but it soon passed. Our landlady was very nice to us. We went to an evacuees' school across the road – we thought we were more intelligent than the other children! But we really enjoyed it. One of our friends there however, had her parents killed in a raid. There wasn't an air raid shelter at the school – we were always told to go straight home. But we were terrors and went to stay with friends miles away!

Our parents used to come down at weekends to see us. One particular weekend, however, we went home to Bristol for a change. When we got back, there had been an air raid on Weston and a bomb had dropped behind our house. That made the ceiling of our house collapse right onto the bed where we'd slept! So we had to turn tail home again. We weren't evacuated again after that, so we stayed in Bristol throughout the whole war.

Our Dad was a commercial traveller, and wasn't called up because of his age. Our parents got married quite late, because in those days the eldest son of the family looked after the parents until they died. They were engaged seven years before they got married, until my mother broke off the engagement and sent him an ultimatum! He was in Newcastle but came flying back to Bristol...

One day an incendiary bomb fell through the roof of the garage at the end of our road. Our car was inside, and there were petrol pumps outside. Dad got inside and put the bomb out before it all blew up, and before anyone else realised that the bomb had been dealt with. It was a common sight, to see people putting out incendiary bombs with just stirrup pumps and a dustbin lid. After a raid the water tanks came around on lorries when the water had been cut off. There was so much comradeship then, people were much friendlier. You knew everybody in the street.

At the end of the war we went on holiday to a farmhouse in the country, and we suddenly heard this dogfight in the sky. Everyone staying in the farmhouse was scared stiff – they'd never seen such a thing before – but it didn't worry us at all, and we went out into the field to get a better look. The enemy plane was shot down in the end. But when we saw the plane crash we though, 'there's somebody dying.' We thought how terrible it was, even then.

CHAPTER 5

EVACUEES

The Evacuation authorities received many heart-rending letters from parents who were most anxious about their children's welfare, yet cowed by the bureaucracy of the evacuation system. The two examples below make astonishing reading and suggest that the rights of parents to even basic information about their evacuated children could often be treated in a most cavalier fashion. (All names and addresses have been changed.)

Mrs Kilroy
7 Hayton Gardens
London SE20

2 April 1941

Dear Sir

I am writing to you on a matter concerning my little children 3 little evacuees at Devon. My little boy states that he has been caned by his uncle for wetting bed is it right for him to do this also to cower children down so that they don't know their own parents. My little boys have got a very flash Billet but their little hearts are breaking. My little girl was in bed ill when I arrived to see her yet I was told nothing, I took my little boy out with me and I had to force him to go back into the house all of the little ones were very upset they were all standing together not allowed to play like other children is this the kind of treatment our little London children deserve I went to the Billeting Officer but he was too busy to see us until today Monday but we were due home then. Can't something more be done for our little ones they want kindness and a good mother to look after them not people who have never had any children of their own. I wanted to bring the little boy back that had been punished but was told I must take the 3 but I did not have enough fare is this Justice, also I had to bring home a child that was ill. My little ones are sweet little mites. They live at:

Mrs Hall
7 Preston Rd
Exeter, Devon

Will you kindly see that my little ones are not punished or hurt any more. I believe my little ones before a jumped up Lady and Gent. My children has only a poor home and should have been put where there is a little kindness shown.

(sgnd) Mrs. Kilroy

172 Welland Rd
Streatham
London   SW16

6.2.42

Dear Sir

I am writing to you to appeal for help in recovering possession of my son William.

He was evacuated roughly a year and seven months ago. He went to a Mrs Green, of 43 Lacey Rd. Exeter, Devon. I was not able to send the boy away with a trunk full of new clothes, as I was at the time receiving help from the Assistance Board, and so I was not in a position to send the boy away as I would have liked.

However, I did my best, and have since sent him as much money and clothes as I could. Just before Easter of last year my husband from whom I am separated (I have custody of the children – Court Order) went to Mrs Green and told her that I did not think it the right thing for my husband to take a strange woman to see my boy, and I sent her the boy's fare and asked her to put him on the train and I would be at this end to meet him as I had not got the money to come myself and fetch him. She wrote back and said she would send him back with her son who was coming to London at Easter. We waited for them, but they did not arrive.

I then wrote again to Mrs Green and asked her why they did not come, as promised. She replied that she had spent the money on the boy and was not going to send him home. Since then I and my daughter have written repeatedly to Mrs Green, without receiving an answer. I have sent money and presents to my boy, without acknowledgement. We have not known whether he is alive or dead, ill or well.

About two months ago I went to the Citizens Advice Bureau, and they got the information for me that Mrs Green had moved from Exeter, Devon, into Somerset but they could not get the address where the boy was although he was still with Mrs Green. They advised me to go to the NASPCC, which I did. The officer said that all he could do in the matter was to try and get the boy's address for me, which he is trying to do. I then wrote to the LCC and explained the position to them and said I wanted my son home. I had no reply directly from them, but I had notice from the Children's Care Committee, 48 Acre Lane, Brixton London. I went full of hope, thinking that now at last I shall get help to get him home. Did I get help? I got insults and abuse in plenty. Help nil.

I was interviewed by a girl, who I should imagine could not possibly have the slightest experience in the care of children much less knowledge of the problems of the parents. She did not know anything whatsoever about my case beyond the fact that my son was in need of certain article of clothing. She had the child's address, but flatly refused to give it to me (as if I were a criminal) instead she gave me the address of the schoolmaster. She called my husband a liar, or words to that effect. She did not know even that I had no knowledge of the boy's whereabouts for over 8 months and do not know where he is at the time of writing except that he is somewhere in Somerset, yet she had the audacity to say my husband is not speaking the truth when he says he has been continually sending money and clothes for the boy.

Now I am writing this letter to you as a last resort.

You are the Head, and I am a poor working class mother who is appealing to you for help. Do please help me. I will pay the boy's fare home, if you will get him sent home for me failing that if you will get me his address I will get the money together to go and bring him home myself.

I do hope you will help me, I will be so grateful.

Yours truly,

(sgnd) Ethel Davies

GERALD SMITH

I can remember Mum coming into the room with a few tears in her eyes, and she had a letter in her hand, and we thought something had happened, a bereavement or something. She read the letter to us and told us we'd been accepted as evacuees to Hartland – that was the place we were eventually going, though we didn't know at the time, obviously.... I had heard on the radio that others had left, and it meant a lot of excitement, because what I had heard about, was that every child seemed to be enjoying it so much! I couldn't understand why mum was so upset about it...

The day we went, it was a nice sunny morning. It was February 19, 1941, and we assembled at Ashton Gate school, all the coaches and all of us kids as they're known today. We were hastily placed inside the coach, with our kitbags and carriers and sandwiches, and we drove down to Temple Meads station. That was the start of our evacuation, which was to be the start of one long holiday. The scene at Temple Meads was very dramatic, because I don't think I can ever remember having been on a train, Now this must have been amplified by almost every other child there, because even getting to Weston was a Sunday School occasion. So there were these hundreds of children along the platform, and chaos seemed to be reigning, although everything must have been so well organised. We must have taken an awful lot of controlling, to get us inside the railway carriages, and safely on our way to wherever it was we were going. We had no idea where. It was the old GWR railway then, and I remember very well nobody seemed to rush for the seats – everyone wanted to be in the corridor, to be running up and down, but the train was so packed. It was all supposed to be hush hush, but I think the whole of Bristol could have heard us from Temple Meads!

We all had our labels around our necks saying where we were coming from – not where we were going to – and of course we all had that cumbersome gas mask hanging around our necks, which took up as much room as half a child in those days. Mums and Dads were stood crying, waving, but with tears flowing from their eyes – and we just couldn't understand that. It was funny – you had to go all year to get just one trip to Weston, and here we were on a train going to somewhere we didn't even know, and we didn't have to go to Sunday School all the year for this one!

The journey took so long in those days, as you might realise, because you had to stop, not necessarily to pick up people. I never understood why we'd stopped, but I suppose it was trains coming in the other direction. But it was an all day journey, although the journey itself was only 120 miles, to Hartland in north Devon. I wasn't on my own, I had my younger brother and sister, but I was on my own when we got to Hartland, because it was unfortunate that there were three of us, and not many people were prepared to take three children into their homes. It was dark and late at night before we were eventually split up. My younger brother and sister were sent some eight miles away to a place called Welcome, and I ended up in Hartland – taken in by a very unhappy lady, who didn't want a young lad intruding into her home. And I remember quite well the police constable ordering her to take me in, saying that the law said she had to take in an evacuee, and I was the unfortunate one, like a ping-pong ball, being batted backwards and forwards.

It wasn't a good start for me... I remember looking out of the window of the room that I was in, and I could just see the sea in the distance, and I thought they'd taken my brother and sister over what was to me then as an ocean – I'd hardly even seen a river – and I cried bitterly because I thought I was entirely on my own. But the great thing was my first night's sleep in lovely white sheets, so fresh. We'd been going down the Portway Tunnel, every night for six months we'd walked there and back from bedminster where we lived, down underneath the Suspension Bridge, and within twenty four hours, to be in a bed, between clean white sheets, and not a sound – it was too wonderful for words.

In the morning, when I woke up, I couldn't believe it. It was nothing but fields, and I found I was on a dairy farm. My book, which I'd read at school about the farmer and his dog, and the green fields – that became a reality over night. And it was tremendous, it really was.

My landlady had come to accept that I was there, and I can understand the annoyance of the routine interrupted, because it was a dairy farm and she washed all the bottles and prepared the delivery of the milk around the little village of Hartland, and I must have been an intrusion. But eventually, I became a very handy person, because I was paid the princely sum of two shillings a week by my step-parents – a Mr and Mrs Jeffries of Parkview, Hartland – that was the actual address – for all my labouring during the week, milking the cows, haymaking, and cutting the corn. It was very enjoyable, but very hard work!

At thirteen that two shillings a week seemed to be a lot of money. If I went short it was because of the coupons. I had the money for sweets, but sweets weren't available. Tooth decay was not a problem then like it is now, I can assure you.

My brother and sister eventually came back into the village, and they went into a bungalow in Hartland – they had a fantastic view. But the funny thing was, people were very disciplined and strict in those days, and they had to go into Hartland Square and do their letter writing on a seat in the square so that they wouldn't upset their ink on the table in the house! That's how fussy they were. We all settled in, and everything became part of everyday life. I wondered afterwards how they managed without us – we did an awful lot of work for them. We also had school holidays – not to go out and play, but to go down the woods, collecting timber for the little school boiler. We enjoyed that as well – anything to get away from lessons.

One of the most dramatic things I remember is the noise of war. Just imagine if you can the noise of a bomb coming down. When we see an explosion now, which is very dramatic and very sad, it is terrible. But imagine hundreds of those in one night – the noise of these explosions, the noise of the ack-ack guns, the noises of the shells exploding in the air – perhaps one of the worst noises of all – the shrapnel raining down and hitting the buildings... dogs barking, shattering glass – this went on all the time. We used to live in Ashton Rd at the time and for the first air raid we taped up the windows as we were ordered to, and I was under the carpet under the table, trembling so much I couldn't keep still. It was the thundering of the bombs. In the morning I looked out over Ashton Park, and you could see all the barrage balloons over Avonmouth. And I remember one night during the blitz – a tremendous blitz – I think it went on for eleven hours, non-stop – and during the blitz there was a thunderstorm. I remember seeing fifty or sixty barrage balloons all coming down burning, all breaking up in the sky – rather pretty now, if you saw it, rather like a firework display, and when I came out the whole of Bristol looked to be on fire – just one red glow from left to right. It was truly fantastic, in its irony.

MRS PERRY

There were twelve of us evacuated to the same boarding house in Perrenporth in Cornwall, and we were there for about eighteen months. Three of us were aged between twelve and fourteen, but the others were all little ones, right down to about three years old. I remember one of the little boys had been buried in a shelter and he was pulled out by his legs. He was a nervous wreck, but we all sort of helped each

Mrs Perry as a teenager during the war.

other. I thought it was wonderful to look after some of these little ones, because I was the youngest of three sisters, you see.

We had food like we'd never seen before – I remember the ladies looking after us had this great big dish of cream on the side. We had bread and jam with cream on top – they used to call it thunder and lightning – and we thought it was lovely. We also had to help make Cornish pasties. Poor old dears, they tried their best with us, but we must have been very hard work. They weren't used to us cheeky London children, and I was said to be the worst of the lot! It was freedom in a way, but I did miss my parents so.

I remember one particular time when we were all sitting out on the porch listening to the *White Cliffs of Dover*, hooting and howling and wanting to go home. We didn't have any contact with our parents, you see. All we heard about was the bombing of London. What I didn't know was that my mother and sister had already moved out of London. This one particular night I was determined to walk home, and I had asked a

London evacuees in Cornwall.

Cornish man which was the road to London – and he said, "That one my dear, but you've got a long walk!" That night, it must have been about twelve o'clock, it was all quiet. I'd got a little bundle of clothes and was ready to go. I'd literally got one leg out of the window and I thought to myself, oh, it is dark! Then there was an old owl that hooted. I shot back into bed. If I'd been lucky enough to have got a lift back home, I would have found the place bombed and my parents gone.

In all, I didn't like evacuation – I think it was the same for most London kids. People thought of us as a bit cheeky and not very nice – they'd call out after us. We didn't have any schooling, because the local schools were all full up with their own boys and girls. It's taken a long while, even now, to catch up on things. I would say I never did any more schooling after I was twelve. We had a lot of nature walks and spent most of our time on the beach. I taught all the little kids to do cartwheels! But Cornwall was beautiful. I've been back two or three times and the house is still standing. It was wonderful just to go back. Every time I hear the *White Cliffs of Dover* I think, lead me to that little bed again. When I look back on it now it seems like I went there a little girl and came back a grown-up girl.

When I came back to Farringdon, where my parents had moved to, it was almost time for me to start work. The problem was that there were no jobs. We ended up with eight of us living in one room. My Gran would sit in a chair with no middle in it, and I remember it was a tough job getting her out of it! To make things worse our stamp cards had been burnt in London, and there was no way of getting work without a stamp card. I was sent to an airforce camp at sixteen and the first work I did was digging an emergency landing strip. Later I cleaned aircraft, sparked plugs, and did camouflaging and things like that. That was in Shellingford between Oxford, Farringdon and Swindon. It was mainly women who worked in the airforce camp.

It was at Farringdon that I met my husband, he was in the Marines camp there. There was an RAF camp, a Marines camp and an American camp. The GIs weren't for me, they were a bit pushy. Mum used to say, "You go to the American base and get me a tin of spam or sweets or something." We three sisters used to dress up in what we had and go. It was difficult finding things to wear though. I remember I had one suit, a black one, with a pleated skirt. I bought the material in a market with my coupons. I had that thing for six years. I was wearing it even after the war, but I used to trim it up different every night with beads, a white collar or embroidery. If we got hold of a bit of parachute we'd make underclothes – we were lucky sometimes, being at an RAF camp.

We had marvellous dancing every night. The American big bands in Shrivenham were terrific! They'd even send lorries out to make sure they had enough girls to dance with – jiving and the like. From the time when I was sixteen to when I was eighteen, at the end of the war, I'd say that was the time of my life.

JAMES HALL

After a twelve hour journey from London we arrived at Shepton Mallet station, unhappy, hungry and bewildered. I was ten and I was with my two brothers, one seven and the five. There were about eighty cockney children all together and we were pushed and shoved into a long line and marched to an assembly room at the top of the town by the Cenotaph.

While we were in there we were given a bag which contained biscuits and sweets, which we soon devoured because everybody was so hungry after the journey. Then people started coming into the hall and taking children away. One of the women tried to take my youngest brother, but I wouldn't let him go as my mother had told me to keep us together. No way did I intend to let him go, so the woman gave up.

After a while this elderly gent came up and said, "Would you three come to the car outside as I'm going to take you to your new home." I said we would, as long as we could stay together. Then the car stopped in Combe Lane and this gent said, "One of you must get out here as we are unable to find anyone to take three boys." I said, "No way! We all stay together." He explained that whoever stayed there, the other two would be just down the road and I was so tired by then that I finally let my brother go.

The car took us just a little further down Combe Lane and stopped. There stood Mrs Stockwell, who said, "Come on boys, you come with me." She took us into her kitchen, which was warm and friendly, and she made us cocoa and sandwiches. We were drinking and eating, then finally I told her about my other brother who'd been taken from the car. "Was there three of you?" asked Mrs Stockwell and she assured me that the next morning she'd find out where he was and have him as well. I realised she was a good woman and felt better about everything. She could see we were tired and we were taken to the bedroom, where we soon fell asleep.

I woke up to the sound of a cockerel crowing and I went to the window and opened it. I'll never forget the sight of those beautiful flowers and fields and the smell of the fresh air. I was really excited and woke my brother up to show him too.

While Mrs Stockwell, whom we called Stock (she didn't seem to mind) was cooking the breakfast, we ran down the lane to where they had taken my brother. The woman there let us in and there were five children, including my brother, sitting having breakfast. I asked my brother if he was all right and he said, "Smashing!"

I told him he was coming to live with us and about the fields and everything I'd seen from my window. I said I was going to take a look and all the kids jumped up to come too and we ran down the lane.

We got as far as Bowlish House and saw the roof of the building was alive with white doves. It was such a beautiful sight to us kids as in London it was all concrete roads and buildings. Then I realised Stock would have our breakfast ready so I ran back with my younger brother while the others went on. We had the quickest breakfast ever eaten and ran off to catch up with the others. We met up with them in Ham Lane, but by that time there were about fifty children and they were calling at all the houses until in the end about eighty cockney kids, who'd never seen green fields and wild flowers, descended on Ham Wood.

The girls picked wild flowers and the boys climbed all the trees and we got this marvellous feeling of freedom. All thoughts of home just vanished. From that day on,

Ham Wood became a favourite with all the evacuees in the area. Everybody congregated there after meals. We made our four-wheeled bogeys and just flew down Ham Lane.

We learnt the name of every bird, wild flower and animal. We also learnt how to milk cows as Mr Allen in Combe Lane was a farmer. We used to hitch up his horses to his milk cart and away he went to the field where he kept his cows, then we started milking. When your bucket was full, you tipped in into the churn on the cart. We got so good at it, Mr Allen didn't bother to come with us. We just took the horse and cart, picking up the kids on the way, made for the cows and milked them. There'd be about twenty cockney kids on the horse and cart, all red faced and singing *It's a long way to Tipperary*, who just six months before hadn't even seen a cow!

One night a German plane which must have lost its navigator came down on its way to bomb Bristol. It had come down so low, it crashed into the hills at Stratton-on-the-Fosse. Word soon got around and it was the done thing then to get souvenirs. Any part of the plane would do.

So eight of us went up there to look and we took an old invalid carriage with us. It had a big basket, two wheels at the back and one small wheel at the front, which you had to steer with a long bar. We arrived at the crash site and saw the plane was a Dornier bomber. Its cockpit was buried in the hillside with the impact. The army had also arrived and placed sentries all round the plane and when we tried to get near the plane to take souvenirs, they fired over our heads. So we all kept a safe distance and finally realised we weren't going to get anything so we made our way home.

All eight of us climbed on the invalid carriage and set off to Shepton, which was downhill all the way. As we picked up speed, we realised that there was no stopping so we just held on. We passed some cars and a bus and I'll never forget the look of the bus passengers as we overtook!

We approached Shepton and at the viaduct in Waterloo Road we turned right into Cowl Street. Everybody was shouting instructions, but we decided to go right to the bottom of Cowl Street and into the entrance of Mrs Linthorne's house as there was a slight incline in her garden where we thought we would stop.

For years the gate to her garden had been open, but what we didn't realise was that someone had shut them that day. We turned left and when we saw the gate shut, a big shout went up and we smashed into the gate. There were bodies everywhere with broken legs, broken arms and cut heads. Shepton Mallet Hospital was like a casualty station. After a few days we came out. Some had plastered arms, plastered legs and crutches and the rest had bandaged heads! But it didn't stop us getting to Ham Wood.

Winter of 1940 was very cold and as it was coming to Christmas, we decided to go carol singing. For two weeks my brothers and I rehearsed our rendering of *Silent Night* until we were voice perfect. We set out on a cold, moonlit night and soon collected a few pennies, which wasn't bad, but we felt it wasn't good enough for all our efforts. So we made our way to Upper Charlton where there was a big house. It was surrounded by six foot privets and the house was covered with ivy. It certainly looked forbidding and frightening. We opened the gate, which creaked, and walked up the driveway while owls hooted in the garden. It seemed an eternity before we reached the front door which was set in a porch. We stood in the porch and I asked my brothers "Are you ready?" They both nodded.

We sang *Silent Night* and when we had finished I grabbed the knocker, which was shaped like a lion, and gave two knocks. We stood back and wondered what was going to happen.

Finally a little old lady answered the door and she asked us in before we could say anything. Her place was full of beautiful pictures and vases and had a lovely carpet in the hall. She took us through to a room where there were about twenty people drinking and eating, who she said were Christmas guests. After we'd warmed ourselves by the big log fire, we were asked to sing *Silent Night* to her guests. We sang it and we were note perfect. The guests stuffed apples and oranges in our pockets and asked us about London while we had tea and cake at the big table. Finally the lady gave us all a ten shilling note, which was a lot of money in those days, and told us to make our way home as it was getting late.

We wished them all a happy Christmas, came out and just ran all the way home. We decided to buy a turkey for Christmas with the money.

We went to Stan Lewis, the butcher in Town Street and ordered the turkey. He threw in the stuffing for free and we had a wonderful Christmas dinner that year thanks to that old lady. Our Mum was staying for Christmas too, so when we'd eaten we sang her our rendering of *Silent Night*.

Gradually the local children would join in our play. At first they had spurned us as if we had a disease! The authorities found us places in all the local schools. I went to Waterloo Road school where Mr Poles was the headmaster. He was held in high esteem by all the evacuees. Another good teacher there was Mr Sparks. He was very strict however, and always soaked his canes in vinegar before he used them. He kept them in a big sweet jar full of vinegar where the whole class could see them. Being so boisterous, the London children often got six of the best. I suffered it myself for climbing over the school wall and not using the gate!

Two years passed with us living with Mrs Stockwell, who was a great woman. We treated her as our own mother, but we finally had to leave. Our mother was bombed out and our home destroyed, so she moved down to Shepton Mallet. She managed to get a house in Cowl Street and we came together as a family again at last.

MR SUTTON

I was ten when the war started. I can't remember exactly when I joined the Boys Brigade, but I seem to have been in it at that time. It was about 1940 when the actual raids started in earnest. As Boys Brigade members we seemed to be attending a lot of funerals. It probably wasn't that many, but it seemed to a young mind to be an awful lot.

I was evacuated when I was twelve from Greenbank Senior Boys School to Cornwall. We were told to go to the school with only one case, and the clothes you stood up in. So your mum would put as many clothes on you as possible, so you could get more stuff in your bag. It was woolly on top of woolly, and I remember absolutely everything being labelled. The double decker buses arrived at the school and our parents were informed that they must say their goodbyes there and then, as they weren't allowed to go to the railway station with us. I can remember being sat on the lower deck of the bus and there were a lot of tearful women there, including my mother. But I wasn't tearful, more full of adventure. I was an only child and I didn't feel the pangs of homesickness until later.

The buses seemed to take an inordinate amount of time to get to the station, because there were a lot of cars and bicycles following – it was all the parents, you see. Anyone who had any transport piled everyone in and followed those buses, which were taking a circuitous route to try and lose them! Finally we arrived at Lawrence Hill station, up Barton Hill way, and a hell of a great long train pulled in. It already had London children on it and we were designated certain carriages. We had our teachers with us and the whole school was meant to stay together as a block.

The journey to Cornwall took six hours in those days so I, as an adventurous lad, went wandering along the train. I got lost and it got to the point where a teacher looked at my label and said, "Where's your crowd?" I whimpered back that I had no idea and he ordered me to stay where I was. So I ended up with the East London children. I'd lost my school!

The East End kids were a wonderful bunch of lads. They'd never seen a cow! They'd never even seen a field! There was this one Jewish lad called Lazarus, he was very well educated and stayed with the minister of the village. I remember every Friday the Jewish boys used to have the Rabbi down and give them their lessons. It was an education for me, because I wasn't used to different sorts of kids. There was such a mixture there. I remember a boy called Henry Cordell, an illiterate – a gentle giant. He was really big, a very strong lad. I lived next door to him in Cornwall and I used to write his letters, and read his letters to him from home. Because he was so big nobody would touch me because Henry was my friend. All I had to say was, "I'm going to tell Henry!" I had power!

We had wonderful schooling while we were down there. I cannot tell you how wonderful the teachers were. One of my teachers could keep a rough class like ours absolutely silent just by telling them a story. He had a weight of personality. He showed me the English language. He was a brilliant teacher. He would have been ideal in a grammar school, but he brought his expertise from the East End of London and I was lucky enough to sample it down in Cornwall!

To be honest, I wasn't keen to get home because I enjoyed it so much in Cornwall, though I grew up very quickly. You get some of these country girls and they make you grow up! I was only about twelve, but I got a few country kisses and rather more besides! It was a shock to me, some of it, but I'd better leave it at that! Another thing I saw down there, which was an eye opener, was how animals were slaughtered on the farm. We boys would have to hold down a pig on a stretcher while its throat was cut. We also had the job of cleaning up all the mess. That was even more of a shock for my London mates. We also took the horses out to stud and watched the servicing of the bulls. I was doing that at a very young age and it was an education. You don't need sex lessons! We even used to see the animals calve and foal. It gave us a respect for reproduction as part of nature.

I also learnt about racism when I was in Cornwall. On Bodmin Moor there was a regiment of Sikh soldiers training with the military. We were given strict instructions that we were not even to speak to them, and they were told that they were not to fraternise with the locals. I've realised since that they were being treated very badly. It's a disgrace really, after all they were good enough to do the fighting for us and then they we weren't even allowed to talk to them. My education broadened in every sense during my evacuation. When I came back I was a bit of a country bumpkin for a while, because I had acquired the Cornish dialect. I think I was teased a bit, but I wasn't a boy to take too much!

My father was supervisor of the fire-watching operations. Everybody of a certain age had to do it. I was about twelve or thirteen, and I had a bike, so I used to go as a messenger to a foundry that was situated in Bellevue Rd. The comedy of it was that we never actually took a message! But I used to get half a crown because I had a bike. I was praying for the sirens to go off so I could dash off and get my two and sixpence. I didn't worry about the messages, all I was worried about was the money, because to a boy in those days that was a small fortune. We used to get sweets for a farthing!

The war years were wonderful for me. There was this feeling of fighting the common enemy, an esprit de corps. Everybody left their doors open, and you could walk in. There was a community spirit that doesn't exist today. My mother had to go out to work because of the low wages my Dad was receiving, so when I came home from school one of the neighbours used to call me in and say, "You're coming in here until your Mum comes home!" There were no babysitters, but people would help each other out.

DR DAVIE

There was a blitz in 1940, and Bristol was really being attacked. The headmaster had to think about this. Our arrangements to evacuate the school to Malvern fell through, so he had a word with Winston Churchill about it. Winston was concerned, also because Queen Mary used to visit a lot. She was moved out of London and based at Badminton during the war, with the Duke of Beaufort. Something had to be arranged for her every day as it had been in London – she used to visit Pembroke Rd, right next to Clifton, to visit the Regional Commissioners, and she used to come to Bath a lot, because she collected antiques: she built up the finances of the Royal Family with her investments. It was impossible to refuse her requests – a great friend of hers was Dr Blackburn in Bristol, whom she used to visit quite a lot. She used to say, "I like that!" – and she had to be given it, whatever it was. So if Mrs Blackburn looked out of the window at 11 o'clock in the morning and saw Queen Mary's huge

Clifton boys at Bude.

Daimler arriving, she'd rush around the house, and push all her treasures into drawers, and under blankets! But there was very much that sort of connection with Clifton.

Clifton College became the HQ of General Bradley. General Eisenhower came to see General Bradley in a particular room in School House, and that is where they laid all the plans for the Normandy landings. So we had to move. I had only just arrived at Clifton from being a master at Haileybury – I'd been invited to build up the biology department – and immediately we had to move to Cornwall.

Just before we left there was terrible bombing. At six o'clock as the boys were going in for a meal, and we were going to dine, the housemaster and myself, in our own hall, we heard the whine of the bombers chucking down incendiaries. Once they saw something aflame, they threw down the high explosives. So we couldn't have a meal at all – we had to go up on the roof and scramble around taking off the incendiary bombs, until one in the morning. It was a strange time in Clifton then. There was one chap having a bath, and a bomb came down and blew him out, naked and black, onto a roof 150 yards away! And a lady whom we knew just around the corner, had opened her front door to see if there was an air raid on. And she saw a bomb coming towards her, bouncing! She rushed out of the house while it bounced into her house, and blew up!

Then whole business of organising the move down began. We took five hundred boys, and all the house matrons were taken with them. There was a resident GP, and the house linen was done by the housemasters' wives. They took it on as a duty – it was part of the War Effort!

When we arrived a plane immediately came over – a German plane – and it was shot down. It was our first experience of being evacuees. We were in these flimsy hotels – really just summer hotels – and they used to rock in the Atlantic storms that we had. There were two boarding houses there – School House and Brown's House. The top rooms were used for the boys to sleep in, and downstairs was used as teaching rooms. There was usually a room at the top which we used as a lecture room. And when school finished, the boys had to do their two preps in the classrooms – one before supper and the second one finished at 9pm. It was the war – nobody made a fuss. I had a room which was about 7 x 8 ft, with a little rail across one corner where I could hang some clothes, a chest of drawers and a dormitory bed with scarlet blankets. That was it. Next door to me, on either side, were boys' rooms in which there were four tiered-up bunks. From seven in the morning until nine o'clock at night I had boys tramping on the wooden floors outside my room.

Our diet was not very good, there was a lot of grumbling about food, with a lot of salt fish, but we just had to get on with it. In fact when we got back to Bristol, I was Hall Warden for a number of years, with this marvellous cateress, Mrs Thomas. I was taking breakfast one morning, sitting up at the top table, and there was obviously a fuss going on at the far end, where a boy was talking to the cateress. She said to this boy, "What's the matter?" "Oh" the boy said "well, you know, this egg doesn't smell!" Mrs Thomas said "I'm here to provide the eggs, not the smell as well!" He'd been so used to eggs that had slightly gone off, I suppose!

The most interesting thing was that due to the teachers who were left being very experienced, the actual level of scholarship and exam results were higher than before we left Clifton and after we returned. The boys just had to get on with their work, and that was it... There were no distractions, no girls' school up the road! Life became monastic. The boys were excited by their games and study, and there was nature all around. The only time I could get away was after 2pm on a Saturday. I was isolated, being a younger man, aged about 30. The other masters were all older – I had nothing much in common with them.

There was no access to an urban centre, and there was no petrol to go anywhere. The Headmaster used to invite people down from London on various subjects – Arnold Haskett on ballet, for instance. So we were culturally in touch, although we were isolated. There wasn't very much to interact with. Bude was a very small town, a holiday town, and people only came down in the summer. But I helped set up a little literary society, and we had plays and concerts. It kept us going.

One of the great things about Clifton was its motto – *Spiritus Inter Aliit* – the Spirit Come from Within. It had a tradition that you could be good at games and scholarship as well.

We also took an interest in the town – we wanted to be associated with the place, and our OTC (Officer Training Corps) joined up with some of the boys in the town, and I used to go off and give them instructions in how to run a signals office. We were in the Home Guard, most of us masters. We had a very good relationship with the boys in the town. There was no friction – we led entirely different lives.

The whole business of teaching science was very difficult. I had to go down to see what space we could have in the local school for chemicals, or where I could have my microscopes, or where we could do dissections for anatomy, and that sort of thing. We had to select out everything to go down there. There were three sixth forms, all doing top-class scholarship work. We had to dig a hole in the ground outside the local school for our tanks of sulphuric acid, and for tanks full of dogfish and other animals for dissection! Then after 4pm, when classes had finished, I used what was the local school's Domestic Science Centre. I then had to get out all my microscopes from the cupboards which were full of saucepans and cake tins. We simply had to make do. When the boys were doing dissections – the anatomy of the frog, for instance – we had plastic boxes, and there was a skeleton of a frog in each of these. We had twenty-five of them, so each boy had one. But that of course meant that I had to boil up the frogs in the Domestic Science Centre, and bleach the bones, and assemble them. I would have to make sure everything worked the day before a Practical. You had to devise experiments for the boys' practical which would work at the time, with the materials available and in the time available – an hour and a half – so that the boys could get back to the hotel for their supper. So it was very hard for me.

We got on with our work and with our games. We had a certain number of fixtures with schools who came down by train – from Taunton, for instance – and King's Canterbury. We had a rapport with other schools and shared their problems, finding out how they coped with things. When it came to the holiday period, we had to go back to be bombed in Bristol, and I had to go back to London, which was being bombed to bits.

A very good and distinguished musician friend of mine, Peter Trankel, who died recently, did this splendid thing. He was head of school, and before we left Clifton and went to Bude, he wrote a huge book with all the details of every house and every department in Clifton. All the names, customs, games and traditions – for example in Brown's House, where I was, next to the hall was a stairway down to the boot-room. And the boot-room in Browns at that time was known as "Little Hell." It was all written down so that we would know how this, that and the other was run when the school got back after the war. It was a very good thing.

The boys were not much interested in the war. Of course, we spoke about it – their parents were in different places around the world – but we just got on with what we had to do. We ignored the war completely. Was there a sense of living through an important era of history? No, I don't think so.

CHAPTER 6

GIs

—

MR HACKER

Some very surprising things happened during the war in Bristol, which today seem hardly credible, but I witnessed them myself. In those days the climate of racism was very strong in the United States. Negro soldiers came over here in large numbers, but they were only given very ancillary jobs to do, transport and that sort of thing. When they got here, they discovered a new found sense of freedom because the British civilian population treated them pretty well as equals to the white American soldiers in terms of being friendly to them. This of course enraged the white GIs and then there was trouble. Many white British girls were going with the coloured men and this inflamed the whites and there were a number of riots. They extended to the suburbs as well, I even saw some in Staple Hill, though on a smaller scale. The trouble was centred mainly in Old Market and Brunswick Square or Portland Square, mostly in central Bristol. Most of the US coloured troops were stationed at a base in Long Ashton, a big transport base, and the whites were in different parts of the city including quite a large detachment at Frenchay Hospital. Frenchay was the 298th US army hospital during the war.

The negroes were not trusted to be in the infantry battalions. It was probably only after the Ardennes campaign – the Battle of the Bulge in 1944 – when the Americans got really worried about the Germans breaking through their lines, that they started to let negro soldiers have guns. They were always frightened of them turning on their officers. It was because of the way the whites had treated them for so many years.

The troubles in Bristol would start when the white and black GIs met up. Perhaps it would be at a dance where both were present, and the white GIs would see a white girl dancing with a coloured G.I., so they'd start a fight and try to throw him out, that sort of thing. This then spread into the streets where gangs of them would go around attacking each other. Generally speaking, the whites got the worst of it. The coloured blokes seemed to be much better at fighting. In fact I've seen American white soldiers crying. I saw one standing in a doorway in the Drill Hall in Old Market crying. Near the top of Old Market by the traffic lights, where Old Market joins West Street it came to quite a nasty situation and standing there as a bystander I remember feeling quite indignant that we were being subjected to this. We felt as civilians that we had no proper protection because many of our younger policemen had been called up and we were relying on what were known as Special Constables. At the disturbance there, they formed a sort of a ring around these troops who were fighting each other and I remember an American officer drew up and tried to quell the trouble and one negro soldier went towards the truck. All American lorries carried a spade and one or two other tools clamped onto the side so they could dig themselves out of soft ground if they got bogged down. One of the implements was an axe. He went to take an axe from the side of the lorry and he was going to swing

*The execution trap door at Shepton Mallet Prison, where many GIs (mostly black)
were executed under U.S. military law during the war.*

it. The white American officers cried out, "Hey, put that back!" and he did put it back and things quietened down a bit.

I remember how awful I thought it was that this should be going on in our own city of Bristol and that we felt so unprotected ourselves as civilians, and they could come and have a go at each other like that, regardless really of the safety of the local people.

There was one incident one day when one escaping from detention jumped on a bus near the bottom of Temple Meads and American MPs (Military Police) fired into the bus. They actually fired into the bus full of civilians. The Special Constables, our only police protection were generally men who were getting on a bit, too old for war service, and it left one feeling very much the unimportant partner of the United States.

I remember standing waiting once, trying to get the last bus home, just off Old Market going back towards Fishponds. It was quite early because in wartime the last bus ran about quarter past ten, and it was a hot summer evening. There was an American soldier standing by me with an English girl and he was discussing the race riots. He said, "Back home we'd just string 'em up from a lamp post." He was talking about one of the coloured men. It was amazing how they brought their racist attitudes from the Southern States over here to a quiet respectable city like Bristol, as it was in those days. Several people were stabbed and it was hushed up, like a lot of other things during the war. I remember one case where a white American murdered an English girl, he strangled her in bed, and in typical American fashion, he was quickly pulled out and tried by their own court. I think we had an agreement during the war that the United States should try their own people in their own courts. Anyway, they brought in some psychiatric reason why he had done this and he was quickly flown back to America and got away with it. But if a coloured soldier did anything, he was for it generally, and many were actually hung on rape charges at Shepton Mallet jail.

My main impression of the whole thing was the unreality of it all. There we were fighting the Germans and there they were fighting each other. I think it was covered up for reasons of morale.

MR WADE, MR JOHNSON & MR CARTER

Jay Cameron Wade:

There was no doubt that black soldiers were treated worse than the whites in matters of justice. We expected it. It was just a carry-over from the United States. We never thought about justice, because we knew there couldn't be any. It was not as if we were being judged by a jury of our peers, or anything. You were judged by your superiors. They had a certain idea about you that they brought from home, and we knew that from day 1. I just thought, 'do what you can, and don't let it upset you. And that's the way you survived it.'

Black service outfits were commanded by men who weren't considered good enough for commanding whites. Many of those officers tried to keep the men intimidated and mistreated. Pardon the expression, but we labelled all those as chickenshit outfits, and looked forward to the day when we didn't have to be in them. We could hear comments from the white troops when they didn't know we were close by, such as at the first shot we'd be running; or that we'd make good night-fighters because we couldn't be seen! Well frankly, we laughed. We were laughing at stupidity.

We didn't feel that we were fighting for anything. There were some who felt they were fighting for their country, and so forth, but those of us who kept up with the newspapers and the media, and were constantly listening to Congress – all those people referring to us as second-class citizens – that sort of rhetoric took all the feelings out of you. So the only thing we could do to survive this was to treat military duty as a job. Just another job. We didn't need emotions or patriotism. But being on convoys, and experiencing some of the excitement of being near the front line, and being away from those stupid officers was a relief, actually. So we looked forward to convoys, because of this one thing. If you were a truck driver, you didn't do anything else. You had to load it and unload it – no manual labour, just drive that truck.

Jimmy Johnson:

We were driving in Germany and had a whole goddam outfit surrender to us – we didn't even know they were there! Goddam, where did they come from? A whole troop – we couldn't believe it. I guess they were just tired of fighting. And I hate to say this, but then I wouldn't take no prisoners. I shot every goddam one of them I could. I don't know why I did it. I had an attitude. Now, that I'm home, and sometimes bad things happen to me, I say, Lord, that's my punishment.

Jay Cameron Wade:

I was hospitalised and shipped back to England. They strapped me into a bed for about two or three weeks. I couldn't move. Altogether I stayed in hospital for about two months. Whenever I got the chance to go out on a pass and meet the English people I did so. The first thing we had to get used to was that the police didn't have guns! We thought, that's crazy! In the United States these people wouldn't last two minutes! But we learnt to really enjoy the English people, because they seemed not to care about the colour of your skin. And most of the force that went to town all had the same impression. On our way back to the hospital we would talk about it, and say, we've never met people like this. They are courteous, nice. They don't flinch, or anything, because we are black. They open their families, their houses to you...without hesitation. This was odd, because we had never experienced such a thing. It gave me the feeling that if it could be like this in the United States, it would be a glorious place to live.

Harry Carter:

At first I wasn't stationed far from a jailhouse, in Shepton Mallet. Some people who were hurt in a fracas or something were treated inside there, in the hospital. It was a terrible place. They used to give them honey buckets (slop buckets) to collect waste and take them to the outhouses. I've been on some horrible detail, but that's the worst I ever had to do.

I remember one or two court martials. A guy was accused of raping an English woman. He wasn't from our outfit. His outfit said that he was playing blackjack – or pitty-pat – and he was present at the time she was supposed to have been raped. But they gave him the court martial – death. You know how it was, it was pretty rough when a white woman was involved. They got real rough. So they took him out of his outfit and shipped him back to the States, and we don't know what happened to him. But we were always being given instructions about that.

Winston Churchill, the Prime Minister, he first made a speech when we came to England: "To all Americans" – you know. He called us all Americans. he said, " Enjoy yourselves while you're here, but watch old Jerry" – that's Hitler's men. He said, with his famous cigar, "You're welcome here. We are going to crush the enemy back. All together, all the Allied Generals. I want you to know that when you are here, you are accepted with all our hospitality. We're sorry you had to come such a long way from home, but we are determined to crush Hitler's war machine!"

But when our outfits were scheduled to go home, we didn't go home with the Sixth Army. I wish I had. They went home on the plane. And we went on the big liberty ships.

Jimmy Johnson:

The Bristol people were great – but the guys were not so happy because we had the women, and the money! How can I put it – you get what you pay for. Although boy, it wasn't much what we were paid. But if you went into town, with a girl, you were in trouble if you didn't have some backup. I can understand it now, but then I didn't know what the hell was wrong. I mean, the women, if they didn't want to be with us, they didn't want to be with us!

There was a ladies house down there, off City Road, run by three coloured girls. One day MPs were waiting for the coloured guys when they came out. Would they have done the same thing if it was white guys coming out of there? I don't want to be a troublemaker, but I know they wouldn't have. So the whole outfit left camp, with our sixers(guns) – we were going to shoot the goddam place up. But before we got out of the damn gates, the MPs (Military Police) got wild, cut off all passes and surrounded the whole camp so we couldn't get off the base.

Some of the guys there, they were really good guys, good soldiers. And you know, they were treated bad, those Southern boys. They'd ask for a pass into town, and they really deserved that pass because they were working hard on the docks all day long, loading ships, coming back in the evening. And it was cold! Oh man, it was cold, with that wind off the water – they had icicles hanging off their butts! There was no way I would have gone out there. And I wasn't allowed to give them one. I got mad, because it wasn't right, they were working like dogs. I was wonderin' what the hell we were doing it all for. And I didn't understand why. Back in Texas I was an engineer, building pontoon bridges, trains, all that. And here I was.

I went on a pass to Wales, and we saw a sign for some wonderful "Welsh Rabbit." So we said, Oh boy! Let's go and get ourselves some of that! So we went into the restaurant and ordered it, and the people came out and brought us toast with cheese! And we said, but where's the meat?

Jay Cameron Wade:

If we married with white people in the States, most of the time black families would accept that, although sometimes they didn't like it because it would cause problems for the children. But there was no racial prohibition, because frankly in all of our backgrounds there is a combination of black and white marriages which brought us here. So that was of no significance to us, the fact that it happened. And I never had any problem relating to any woman, white or black! I think my parents' influence on me caused me to really love women. The English man – how can I describe it? He was more complacent than anything. It was amusing to watch him, because these gentlemanly soldiers were something I wasn't used to. I thought soldiers were rugged, uncouth, uncaring... but these English guys had good manners and good behaviour. You couldn't dislike them, but also we could see why they wouldn't be attractive to a lot of women. They seemed to treat women in a matter of fact way. No romancing in the way we were used to doing. Actually, when it came to competing for the same woman, we knew we would win every time. We had all the charm, and could tell all the lies that were necessary! The English just could not tell such a lie. It was interesting... sometimes we felt sorry for them.

When we got back to the States, many black soldiers got ridiculous treatment, which they remember to this day – more than the battles which they'd fought. To have been treated so well by a foreign people in a foreign country, it was a shock to come back and know that these things still happened. We knew we had a battle to fight at home which was worse than any of those on the battlefields of Europe. There, we knew who the enemy was. But with segregation and discrimination, you had so many people doing that, and in such a way that unless you could see what was going on, you wouldn't have known it. They could do it so politely, so deceptively. Sometimes they would put a hand on your shoulder, and speak to you as if they were doing you a favour... but they would be leading you down a dread path. So we had to learn to understand discrimination, and how to counteract it.

I have a list of two thousand, two hundred and forty-one names. That is the original list of all those black soldiers who served. About half of them have deceased over the years. We were denied a part in the victory parades, we weren't on television, we were denied the privilege of participating in that after World War II. We want the president and the Defence Department to do something: perhaps a statue in Memorial Park. I want recognition for what we did, for those of us who were the ones who started integration in the armed forces in the United States.

MR JAMES HALL

I had to get up early in the mornings to do my paper round and one morning I was approached by a soldier I thought looked like an officer. He said, "Hi boy, what town is this?" I realised I had met my first Yank. The Americans had arrived and 6000 of them were posted around Shepton Mallet. They turned the town upside down!

The nights were like a rodeo. All the pubs were full and the money flowed like water. All the girls were snapped up and a good time was had by all. They were generous and us kids had parties thrown for us. They couldn't do enough for us Cockney kids. They were fascinated by our accents and gave us rides in their jeeps and packets of chewing gum to take home.

The only time they were sad was when one of the Americans was hanged in Shepton jail and there were a lot hanged there. They always hanged them at two in the morning after everybody had had a good drink. Many of the guards fainted when they carried out the hanging. The day before any hanging and the day after, the town felt like a morgue. The Yanks felt bad about hanging one of their own boys.

They repeatedly told me that they didn't ask to be in the war. They carried out the hangings for murder at 2.00am, but for rape and stealing of government property, they were shot by a firing squad at 6.00am. I know all this because we were good friends with the Master Sergeant of the jail, who was a great fellow.

CHAPTER 7

FROM EUROPE TO THE WEST COUNTRY

CHARLES HANNAM

I was brought up in Essen, which is an industrial town. My family had been settled there for at least a hundred and twenty years and before then had come from a small village in Westphalia, in north-western Germany. Jews were not allowed to own land in nineteenth century Germany, so they were butchers. Oddly enough, butchery and money holding went together, and so my grandfather set up the Hirschland Bank. It's an interesting thing that the Germans were always accusing the Jews of being rootless and just drifting around. Yet I remember one day in class the teacher asking whose parents were raised in Essen and lots of hands went up. Then he asked who had both sets of grandparents from Essen, and then great grandparents, and still my hand went up when lots of others didn't. Many Jewish families had lived in the same area for hundreds of years.

One of my great-grandparents was a very successful financier whose family were referred to in my family as 'the other Hirschlands' They were really baronial in their style. The whole family became very established in the town. My uncle had even donated an eye hospital to the town and then when the Nazis took power in 1933, they knocked off a stone plaque dedication to him.

When I grew up we weren't very orthodox Jews. We went to the Synagogue on Friday evenings but the dietary rules weren't kept too strictly, except by my grandmother. I knew very little of the persecution to begin with. One time I remember a child shouting in the street and my nanny seeing him off, but there was nothing much worse than that. Then gradually it was like a net closing in. The harassment increased, little by little. I went to a Jewish primary school and then to a Gymnasium, which is like an independent grammar school. They had a quota so that they could only take in a certain number of Jewish kids. I remember my father pleading for me to get in, and I felt terribly embarrassed that he had to plead. From then on things got worse, mainly because the teachers got worse.

Some of the teachers were decent and some were not. They would start by making snide remarks. I remember one day a teacher coming in when the class was being a bit noisy and him saying 'Anyone would think this was a Jew's school.' Perhaps Jewish children were supposed to be especially noisy, I don't know. One of the worst experiences was when one of the teachers, who was a very keen territorial army man, said we could all go on a visit to the barracks to see what happened there. We were all supposed to pay a mark for the trip and when I offered my mark, he said, "Oh no, Jews can't go." They always tried to make you feel inferior. After the war, one of the teach-

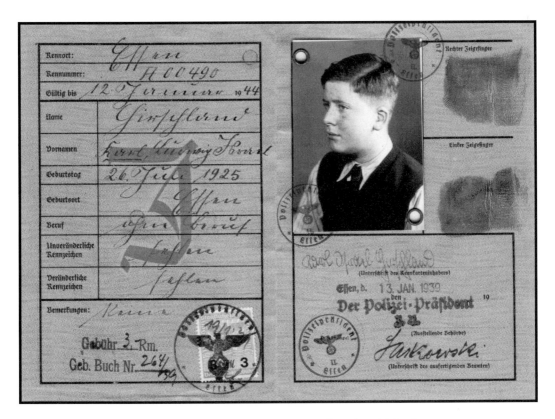

*Charles Hannam's passport stamped with a 'J' for Jew,
with which he escaped the Reich in 1939.*

ers at the school wrote to me in England, asking me to testify that he had never been anti-Semitic...

In many ways I was inferior, in the light of the Nazi ethos for fitness, which is so apparent in many of the old German films of that time. I was a very fat boy, tough enough, but I couldn't do all the required physical activities in the gym. So my father took me to an old boxer, a marvellous man called Herr Kohler. He taught me lots of little things, apart from boxing, like how to climb up a rope. No one had ever bothered to teach me before and I used to just hang there like a lump of lard! You know what gym teachers are like, probably the world over, mine kept on hitting me with the end of a skipping rope saying, "Get up, get up," and yet had he spent three minutes showing me that you put feet round the rope and pull yourself up, I would have done it. I also learnt how to box and later I became very good at it. My boxing career became very useful to me!

My family were not Zionists, who looked to a God-ordained homeland in Palestine. They very much thought of themselves as Germans. I've an awful feeling they might even have co-operated with the authorities if they'd been allowed to. A lot of them had fought in the First World War, and several of them had been killed. They were very patriotic Germans. Uncle Eric had had an Iron Cross for bravery, (First Class), and they just could not believe what was happening. My father probably could have got out of Germany if he'd tried earlier, but several things happened to prevent him. My mother died in 1936 or 1937 from some obscure skin disease and it seemed to take the will out of him, the will to carry on. He said things like 'I haven't got any money abroad'. Now most of the cleverer people smuggled their money out if they had any. He was too law abiding, such a good citizen. I don't think he'd ever smuggled a mark out of the country. The other Hirschlands had got all their Van Goghs and Rembrandts out. Well, they were lucky in one sense, in that Goering confiscated their art treasures and they were put in a safe place, in a salt mine in Bavaria. They got everything back and lived very well. So we weren't the lucky branch of the family.

In 1938 came Kristallnacht, when the S.A. men came and smashed the house up. For me that was a really horrendous experience, because my father was hidden in the attic, and they were known to have burnt houses down. Ours was a detached house with some trees and garden all round it, making it relatively easy to burn down without causing any damage to other houses. I dare say if they'd found my father they'd have beaten him or something, but he was well hidden upstairs and I showed them round the house along with my old grandfather. I'd say, 'Here is the kitchen' and they'd go in and trash everything, knocking off plates and throwing everything about. They were allegedly looking for weapons. I was very frightened as I was only thirteen; it was just after my Barmitzvah. One of my best Barmitzvah presents had been a camera my father gave me and one of the S.A. men just stamped on it and destroyed it. I remember going up to the officer in charge and saying, 'Look what they've done to my camera', I was in tears and he took me by the scruff of my neck and pushed me away. He didn't actually hit me, nobody got beaten.

They finally went away and then the S.S. came. They were a bit more intelligent. They said they weren't going to burn the house down as they wanted houses like that, they'd be very useful. They obviously had a clearer picture of what they wanted and didn't just go round smashing everything. Then the police came and did nothing except shake their heads and walk out again. In the morning my father came out of hiding from the attic and I think that was the moment he realised how bad things had become. So I was sent to England.

This was when the Kindertransport happened. My father took me to Cologne and I had a label put on my coat lapel, and carrying one suitcase with a label I was put on the train for England. A list had to be made of everything in the suitcase and my father had to pay for everything in the case. A pair of shoes which was alleged to be depriving the Germans of a pair of shoes, he had to pay whatever you paid for a pair of shoes. This applied to shirts, trousers, everything. You had to pay a 'fine' on all of it. Of course people were even made to pay their train fares to the extermination camps so this pales in comparison to that, but it was still dreadful. The last time I ever saw my father was at the station in Cologne before I came over to England.

I still remember how yellow everything seemed to me when I arrived at Victoria Station, this strange yellow lighting. I suppose it must have been a fog. I was sent first to a hostel in Ramsgate, and that closed when the war broke out. It had been supported by Jewish professionals. It was a very good place except that we were supposed to be learning English and we didn't learn a thing. We just cleaned the house. I remember cleaning the staircase every morning, as I started suffering from housemaids knee, and then we just mucked about the rest of the day. During this time I still received regular cards from my father, but these stopped as soon as the war began.

When the hostel closed down I was sent to an approved school. Remember, the whole country was in a bit of a panic at the time. The approved school was run by the Home Office and they probably thought we had to be housed somewhere, so they sent us there. All they said to us was, 'Pack up your things and get on the bus. You're going to be trained as farm workers.' There was an export from a lot of institutions, even Barnardos, where children were trained as farm workers and then sent off to Australia or Canada where they were sort of sold off to farms.

I spent six weeks turning the handle of a potato sorting machine, and we just beat each other up and mucked about. It was pretty gruesome. It probably wasn't as bad as all that, but I'd come from a fairly comfortable environment, and I was very miserable there. Some of the older boys had already spent time in concentration camps and wanted to hang themselves. In the first wave of arrests after Kristallnacht these boys had been kept in concentration camps for about six weeks and then they were told to get out, after having to sign a document to say they'd been treated well. They were told they had twenty four hours before they'd be fetched back again. So of course they got out of Germany, only to find themselves in this place in England that looked just as bad, as it had barbed wire all round the huts. I think this was actually to keep the English boys off us, but it still looked very sinister. Although morale was very low, I felt that was where my education really began. One of the best friends I had there had been a medical student before he came over, and I remember cutting kale at five in the morning and being told all about Freud.

My sister, who had come over to England a short while before me, was then working as a German housemaid for an admiral. She was sacked shortly afterwards because an admiral couldn't have a German maid with the war on, so she had found another job. She realised things were getting pretty grim for me at the approved school and although she was only seventeen, five years older than me, she went down to the town and went to see the headmaster of the little grammar school there, a minor public school called Midhurst. She told him she had this little brother who was very unhappy and asked if he could come to the school. Now it so happened that the headmaster, a man called Luke, was an amazing man, a socialist and what you would now call a progressive educationalist. He said, 'All right, send him along.' When I think about how old she was at the time I'm amazed at her resourcefulness. She had even found funding for my tuition fees at the school from an Aunt Ell of the 'other Hirschlands', the ones with all the money in America. It was about £48 a term I think. The head waived the boarding fees. So off I went by train, the envy of the remaining refugee boys at the approved school. I knew hardly any English and communicated with sign language, just showing people my ticket.

Once I started at the school, I tried hard and did well, I think because I realised the alternative would have been potato sorting! I was very conscious of costing other people money while I was at Midhurst and it was embarrassing. I think you're much more proud when you're poor and so I was uncomfortable with the situation and I worked as hard as I could. In the end I got a place at Cambridge, but I couldn't stand being indebted any more, so I volunteered for the army.

Meanwhile I stayed with my sister, who, incidentally had married the brother of Aunt Ell. She had met him when she went to collect my school fee cheque from him. She kept telling me not to spend money and to be really careful all the time I was at school, which is of course the kind of thing you can't stand as an adolescent. Others might say how great it was of me to join the army, but I saw it as a release. And there was enough to eat! School food was appalling compared with army food.

When I finished my training I was called into a tent on the Norfolk coast, and my commanding officer said, "Look here, if the Germans catch you with a name like that, they'll shoot you. We'll have to change it. So what do you want it to be?" We were standing in a tent with the wind howling around us and I had to think of another name. The founder of the grammar school I'd been to was called Gilbert Hannam and I wanted to keep the 'H', so that became my name. The Karl just changed to the English, Charles. Obviously my accent must have disappeared somewhere along the line, so I just went underground and never told anybody anything about my background. When people asked where I was from, I'd just say 'Sussex' because that's where the school was and if people noticed I spoke German rather well, I'd just say I'd had a German nanny.

I came to the war fairly late and I ended up in Burma. It's a very unheroic tale. We saw some Japanese once which was a terrifying experience, except by that time the Japanese were starving and in rags and tatters and we totally over-estimated their strength. I don't think they needed to drop the bomb on Hiroshima, but we cheered when we heard because it meant the war was over, and we'd been about to land in Malaya to start fighting, so of course we were all relieved.

When I came out of the army I went to Cambridge to study history. I taught for a few years afterwards and then came to work at Bristol University. I liked it so much, I've lived in Bristol ever since.

After the war, I found that my father and grandfather had been sent to the ghetto at Theresienstadt. My grandfather had died soon after arrival and my father lasted until one week before V.E. day, which is terribly sad. We know about this because the Germans kept meticulous records of everything, including the people they killed. My wife and I visited Theresienstadt, in the Czech Republic, a few years ago. It's about twenty miles outside Prague and was an old military barracks. There they were, volume upon volume of people who died in the ghetto. We looked up my father and my grandfather in the books and my wife found it so distressing, she was overwhelmed. Just imagine, he spent four years there in terrible conditions, four to a bunk bed. It was the first time I realised how dreadful it was, because even if you didn't go, every day you had to look at the list to see if your name was on it to take the train from Theresienstadt to Auschwitz. Imagine living in that fear. Theresienstadt was supposed to be a model camp; it was the only one the Swiss Red Cross were allowed to visit. Apparently even the same night after the Swiss visit, they had the usual clear out of people to Auschwitz. The Swiss say now that they weren't fooled at all, but that they thought if they said anything, it would get much worse. It was a dismal place.

In the seventies, there was an attempt to set things right back in Essen where we had lived. They were going to name a square after the family: Hirschland Platz. But I could never go to it. It just seems such a cop out.

(For a fuller account of Charles Hannam's wartime experiences, see *A Boy in your Situation* listed in the Recommended Reading section at the back of this book.)

HELEN BIRD

I was just thirteen when the war started. I lived in Duisburg, which is where the River Ruhr joins the River Rhine – the industrial heart of Germany. It was an inland port, and so a target for peak bombing. In fact, the very first bomb that was dropped on Germany was dropped at the end of our road! There was an enormous factory where the Germans converted coal into petrol, which wasn't really a factory – it was just a mock thing, a dummy which looked like a factory. So it attracted a few bombs before they found out that it wasn't the real thing, which was actually a few kilometres away.

*Helen Bird on her first communion day,
with her family before the war.*

I went to school in Duisburg, and experienced three schools which were destroyed – to our great delight! Luckily nobody was in them at the time – part of our schooling was spent in an air raid shelter underneath the school. We weren't told a lot about the war, because we were living it. We spent most nights in air raid shelters; not immediately, but from 1941, when the bombing escalated. Eventually, after the third school was bombed, the whole school was evacuated to southern Germany, to a lovely town in the Schwabenland where I did my Abitur (A levels.)

Mine was probably a unique position, because my father was head of a technical college, and he was the only head in the entire district who did not join the Nazi Party. I think it was in 1932 when my father realised that a lot of people would vote for Hitler, so he decided not to vote at all. When suddenly, a big, black car drew up outside the house, and two SS men jumped out and forced my father into the car and took him to the polling station. But my father found the courage to put his cross against the only other candidate on the voting paper – a token figure. Then the SS man leaned over him and said, "I think you have made a mistake", and forcing the pencil back into his hand, made him put the cross against the Nazi candidate. When you multiply this by – I don't know – perhaps thousands of cases...

The Nazis were seen as a thuggish party by normal decent people. They had all these awful street fights. In our part of Germany were a lot of miners who were Communists and had fought the Nazis in the late 1920s. There were regular street fights, and at the end of our road a Brown Shirt (S.A. man) was actually killed. A monument was erected to this hero, this martyr to the Nazi cause. But later on they found out that he was actually a Jew. This embarrassing discovery happened with the street names, too. We had a Kaiser Wilhelm Strasse (Emperor William St.), and that was turned into Markus Pafratstrasse – because they were two Nazi heroes... and again it was found out later that one of them was actually Jewish! So they had to change the name back again.

But it was a dangerous, crazy situation. Even literature was forbidden – poets like Heinrich Heine, who was born in 1798! But he was a Jewish writer, you see. Anything written by Jewish writers – Thomas and Heinrich Mann, for example, and by people who had emigrated – was forbidden. Even the textbooks in school were slightly altered. Whereas everyone knew that the famous song about the Lorelei on the Rhine – which was almost like a national anthem – was written by Heine, it suddenly appeared in the textbooks as "Poet Anonymous."

Lots of Germans say how they didn't join the Party, but I was in the Hitler Youth, because one had to be. From the age of ten you were just a member whether you liked it or not. So I lived a dual existence – at school I was in the Hitler Youth, but at home my father had a lot of contacts so he knew that we could never win the war. We began to realise that there were things like concentration camps, because one of my father's colleagues had actually been in one. They were not, in those days, exter-mination camps – they were camps to turn 'bad' Germans such as Communists etc. into good Nazis. My father's friend was a socialist, and they were on the Nazi black-list because obviously they were against the Nazis. Even strong Catholics opposed the Nazis for religious reasons. We had a wonderful bishop – Von Galen, Bishop of Munster – from one of the old aristocratic families in Germany. He spoke out strongly against the Nazis, right from the word go – really stuck out his neck – when he found out that mentally subnormal people were killed in institutional homes. This happened during the thirties and forties, because the Nazis didn't want to feed anyone who wasn't useful to the community. But I think even the Nazis did-n't dare to touch him, because he was very well known abroad. So we knew – because we were Catholics, as most of the Rhineland was – a bit more than the rest of the community.

As the war progressed there was a strong suspicion about what was going on in the camps, but one didn't know how horrific it was. Most of the concentration camps were either not in Germany, or very much hidden. I don't think the guards dared to open their mouths when they came on leave. It's difficult to explain, because the pro-paganda in Germany – with Teutonic thoroughness – was really all pro-Nazi. There was only one newspaper, which was controlled, there was one radio station, which was controlled. Mail from abroad hardly ever came in – if it did it was censored and crossed out. And one was afraid. If one knew something, one kept quiet. Now that is not very heroic, but I've tried to explain to people – you can't suddenly turn 80 million people into heroes and heroines. Most people tried to lead an ordinary life. Perhaps 10% did something – stood up... and suffered. And perhaps 10% were really cruel Nazis. But then you still had 60 million people who were trying to keep living.

In Cologne there was a large Jewish population. Most of the Jews in my town were actors, lawyers, journalists – and quite a few of them managed to get abroad before the war really started. My uncle had a wonderful patisserie and cafe in Cologne, and he really supplied the vast Jewish community with bread. It was one of the better areas of Cologne, with lovely villas which belonged to Jewish families who had been there for years, all their lives, as had their parents, and grandparents. Some of them had been there since the time of Frederick the Great. They thought they were Germans first and Jews second.

My uncle was very good. He supplied them even when things were difficult. He'd show them the back way into the shop. He actually finished up with an ape: one of his Jewish customers had a huge ape, as a pet. Then he emigrated, and left my uncle with this ape! Peter was its name, but he couldn't live on carrots and cabbage – he obviously needed oranges and bananas, and there weren't any, so he got terrible skin trouble, and very aggressive. He was a huge animal, and lived in an outdoor cage and an indoor cage. My uncle could do anything with him, but eventually he was afraid that the house might be destroyed during an air raid, and thought that Peter might get loose from his cage, and probably kill someone. So when one of my cousins came home on leave he was eventually shot, and it was like a bereavement in the family.

One had to be very careful – I could never repeat what was discussed at home. It was very dangerous. I came home one day to find all the books in my father's bookcase strewn all over the floor. The SS had walked in, looking for forbidden books. But the bookcase is a very big piece of furniture – I still have it here, against the wall – and behind the front row of books one can hide a lot of others.

My father was often 'called away' by the local Nazi chief, because some of my father's students actually split on him, reporting that "this man has said we can never win the war" or that "there is good and bad everywhere..." Father was a very tolerant and liberal man, and he was warned on many occasions. The Nazis really ruined his life. After the war a list was found, and my father's name was at the top of it for immediate extermination had Germany won the war.

No sooner did I get home from being an evacuee than I got my call-up papers. I wanted to go to university, but I wasn't allowed to because I hadn't done any military service. Everybody had to do one year – the famous "Arbeitsdienst" – community service. In 1944 I went to an awful labour service camp in northern Germany, on the Baltic sea. It was terrible. I had to get up at 4am and help the local farmers dig potatoes or cut sugar beet. I hated it because I wasn't very strong, and I'd always lived in the city. And then I made myself so unpopular because I felt the war was really getting towards its end, and that we had to do something about it. We just wanted to escape, basically. Some of the girls with me had the same ideas, and obviously it was reported, that I was spreading rumours. By then of course the plot on Hitler's life had unfortunately failed, although we had all hoped it would succeed. It was 20th July 1944. So they gave me a punishment posting, and sent me to Berlin, where I was involved with the Luftwaffe.

I was attached to an anti-aircraft unit, surrounded by gunners and huge, big, anti-aircraft guns. I worked some complicated apparatus: a range-finder, which was like a huge box set with lots of binoculars pointing inwards. A set of dials very accurately reflected the distance to the enemy plane and the angle that our missiles should be fired at to hit them. That information was automatically transferred to the guns. It was very technical and highly developed, extremely accurate. These binoculars so enormously magnified the planes that one could sometimes see the bombs starting to fall, and we knew where they would fall, and how close by. But I don't think I was very good at my job: I can assure you that I was never personally involved in shooting down a plane!

I wasn't the only one doing this, there were several girls. It was extremely dangerous since we were right out in the open, because they thought this was one way of getting rid of those not toeing the line. But in spite of the danger, I thought I was in paradise because I was surrounded by men! Most of them were elderly gentlemen, or very young boys, but at least one was in a community again. Sometimes a lot of women together can get very bitchy, and some of the leaders in our camp had obviously been really tough, hard Nazis. Cruel... They were educated, not fools, but they had become so fanatical in their views, that they still thought that there was some way this glorious Nazi machine could change the war. By then of course we had heard about the new weapons, and that the atom had been split. But the men in Berlin were charming, and helped us, although it wasn't a very nice existence, living in cold barracks, with very, very little food – but at least one felt among friends.

I was in Berlin until Easter 1945. By then my parents had left their house, which had been bombed. My father was very ill, and was evacuated into central Germany – the Harz mountains. Somehow I found out where they had got to. I can't explain it, but in May I suddenly felt that if I didn't leave Berlin that day I would never ever get home and see my parents again.

I went to see my CO and told him. He said, "I wish I could let all my girls go, because I know you will be in big trouble once the Russians come. But we will just pretend that your father has died, and I'll give you a three-day permit to bury him. If you get caught, you know that you will die as a deserter, and I shall probably die as well."

Celebrating Christmas 1945 in a friend's house, which still had a roof.

So six of us let our fathers and mothers "die" and we left Berlin. I actually got out on the very last train that went towards the west in May. Hitler was still alive, in his bunker, and the SS were absolutely ruthless. There were controls everywhere. It's a miracle that I got onto the train, considering my permit had been scrutinised by four different people, who obviously felt there was something fishy about it. If it hadn't been for some commotion on the platform, to which the last SS guard's attention was diverted, I don't think I would have got onto the train.

But I did get in, and the train left – although it didn't get very far. An American plane had put the locomotive out of action. We all jumped out, and from then on I just walked. I don't know how long it took – you can't imagine the chaos. There were people walking everywhere – women, children... and of course German soldiers running away from the east, trying to get the west.

The terror of being left at the mercy of the Russians was partly a feeling of guilt – because we knew our troops hadn't always behaved impeccably. One knew from people who came home on leave, and also rumours abounded. It was quite obvious that once the Russian army swept over Germany, they would take their revenge. Also, some of their troops – not the crack troops – they were good – but some of them would swarm all over the country on funny little horses, and of course they hadn't seen women for years, and obviously had lived in rural areas. Then they thought all the women were just there for them. Some of them were completely uncivilised, and the raping of women really was tremendous. It really was. That is not a story. They had a completely different attitude. They were thousands of young Russians who had been conscripted, and actually of course had liberated their country. But obviously they had suffered – suffered an awful lot. It's not very easy to be magnanimous when you've been at the receiving end for years.

I got into the Harz mountains the night before the Americans arrived. We were reunited, and found ourselves stuck in this village for some time. Eventually, a wonderful British officer, who knew that this part of Germany was to be handed over to the east in exchange for free access to Berlin, helped the local people to get transport to the west. So we got home – with the help of the British army.

The house was still there – at least the walls and floor were still there – there was no roof, windows or doors! We made do with our cellar. I gradually stripped the lino off the kitchen and nailed it to the rafters, and so we had one room enabling us to live again – or exist. The food situation was dreadful. The English Quakers, however, were wonderful – they supplied us, their enemy. I thought this was wonderful. We had some ration cards for just the bare essentials, and one wasn't even sure of getting that. We queued up every morning, hopefully. But we managed; and a flourishing black market developed.

At the end of the war there was hatred for the Nazi Party. There were still some fanatics – who are probably still around today, in their eighties and nineties. There was a general realisation then where the blame lay, and what had led to this awful catastrophe.

A Nazi meeting in 1939.

Then I wanted to go to Heidelberg University – but it was very full, so I was accepted at Cologne. My best friend, who had been accepted at Heidelberg, but was waiting another year, took an interpreter's post at my future husband's office. He was from Bristol, and was in Germany in the Control Commission. This was an organisation set up at the end of the war to find men and women who could help the German Authorities get back to normality, and establish a new kind of democratic government. Most of the Germans that had not been killed in the war had been Nazis in positions of authority who were now in hiding, sacked or demoted – no longer in office, thank God. There was suddenly a need for people who could take over and create some stability out of this chaos. There was no rail link, no telephones – it was a shambles. The Commission drew on men who had been in the forces. Dickie – my husband – was not a military man: he was in the Royal Engineers. They were extremely useful for advice on building again. All the bridges across the Rhine had been destroyed, for example, so they built pontoon bridges. Dickie, with some German staff, was in charge of a huge transport unit, so those who did the building had some transport.

On her 21st birthday my friend invited him and several other people from the office to dinner. I found myself as his partner at table, and I could sense that he was terribly lonely. He lived in an officer's mess. By then the non-fraternisation ban had been lifted, and I gave him my parents' address. They made friends, and gradually as I came home from university we became friends too. He could see that we were struggling, and so he helped very tactfully: when he left, there was sometimes a tin of corned beef hidden somewhere, or a packet of cigarettes...

When I came to Bristol with him, I loved it. My first impression was that there were more houses in Bristol that were still standing than at home – don't forget that Cologne was 90% destroyed, and I just couldn't believe that there were whole streets which were still there and intact! And everybody was so very friendly. I have never come across anyone who made things awkward for me. So I thought, I think I could live here quite cheerfully, although as a matter of fact I would have lived at the North Pole with him by then!

Bristol was my new home. I was so fed up with nationalism and patriotism – it meant nothing to me.

154

MR HEINSDORF

I came from an Austrian military family – my brother was in the army, and my father was, because he had been a sergeant-major in the 1914-18 war. Naturally, I wanted to be the same. What else was there to do at home? I went to a military school, and before I was sixteen I was sent to the Russian front, to Stalingrad. At that age, you didn't know what you were going out for or what you were facing. The cold that I experienced... it was 46 degrees below zero. How I got out I don't know. But I was in a panzer division, so the chances of getting polished off were less than the poor bugger in the infantry. We were more protected from enemy fire. But our company was 120-odd, and only 27 of us got out. I got wounded out there.

We were re-grouped, and they sent us out to Italy, over the Brenner Pass in the mountains. We were sorting out the partisans – it was not very pleasant. I only had two stripes on my arm yet it was all – "Capitano, capitano!" to them. They give you all the bullshit during the day, but during the night they popped you off. It was the war. There is nothing fair in war. Survival, and that's it... And on the front line, you'd know where the enemy was, but when you were up in the mountains – and don't forget, they were in their own territory – two blokes could knock hell out of ten of yours, and still come out laughing.

Then we went down to the other side of Rome – that's where the front line was. All of a sudden, everything came to a stop. We were loaded into railway trucks and sent back up to the Western Front, because the Yanks, Canadians and British had landed. I got wounded again, and captured in Germany, and sent to a POW camp in Belgium. Terrible, it was. But luckily, I was an outpatient by then, because the British were coming over the Rhine, the Russians were coming the other way into Saxony and Thuringen – there was hell flying either way on the radar. The Russians were coming a bit too fast for my liking, so I got a pair of crutches, nicked a motorbike – and looked like Mickey Mouse in a wheelbarrow, with my crutches by the side of the motorbike – I thought that when the petrol runs out, at least I've got my crutches! So I went west. The wound broke open again – I had a bullet wound in my leg, and had to go into hospital. Then the Yanks came in, and said, "Let's go, buddy, let's go!" The next thing was, my friend and I became ballast in the cargo hold for a troopship. Their wounded were on the top deck. It took twenty seven days from St. Nazaire to the States, where I was a POW for two years. I ended up in Louisiana where we were cotton picking, fruit picking. I was lucky, being allowed to go out to work.

FRONTPOST

NR. 12. WOCHENBLATT FUER DEUTSCHE SOLDATEN 19. JANUAR 1944.

Durchbruch zum Westen der Pripetsümpfe

Grosse deutsche Gegenoffensive östlich von Winniza

Am 18. Januar meldete Moskau, dass die Russen im Norden und im Süden der Pripetsümpfe weiter vorrückten. Im Norden überschritt die Heeresgruppe Rokossowsky nach der Eroberung von Mosyr (14. Jan.) die Ippa nordwestlich von Kalinkowitschi. Im Süden stiess die Heeresgruppe Watutin von Sarny aus fächerförmig vor und besetzte Kostopol und Wladimirsk (s. Karte). Westlich von Nowograd-Wolinsk wurde die Stadt Tuschin, 25 Km. vor Rowno, genommen.

In den Pripetsümpfen versprengte deutsche Einheiten werden von russischen Partisanen, Fallschirmjägern, Flugzeugen und Kosaken verfolgt.

Weiter südlich setzte die Heeresgruppe Manstein starke Panzerverbände in einer Gegenoffensive östlich von Winniza und in der Gegend von Uman ein. Dadurch soll die Bahnlinie Odessa-Warschau geschützt und zugleich die Kontrolle über die von Smjela nach Westen führende Eisenbahn zurückgewonnen werden. Bei Smjela befinden sich die Ueberreste der deutschen Armee, die vor einer Woche von der Heeresgruppe Konjew schwer geschlagen worden war.

Wie die deutschen Offensiven vom Juli und November 1943, so ist auch Mansteins Gegenoffensive zu einem Ringen zwischen deutschen Panzern und russischer Artillerie geworden.

Die OKW Berichte vom 17 und 18. Januar meldeten weitere heftige russische Angriffe längs der ganzen Ostfront, — nördlich des Ilmensees, nordwestlich von Newel, südöstlich von Witebsk, nordwestlich von Kirowograd, und nordöstlich von Kertsch. Von der Leningradfront meldet Moskau einen russischen Einbruch südlich von Oranienbaum.

BULGARIEN UNTER DRUCK

Die deutsche Nachrichtenagentur «Transocean» berichtete am 14. Januar, dass der bulgarische Innenminister die Evakuierung Sofias angeordnet hat. Amerikanische und britische Kampfflugzeuge hatten kurz zuvor auf die bulgarische Hauptstadt zwei schwere Angriffe ausgeführt. Meldungen aus Ankara zufolge befindet sich Sofia in einem Zustand völligen Durcheinanders.

Der amerikanische Aussenminister Cordell Hull hat das bulgarische Volk gewarnt: «Wenn Ihr das sinkende Schiff Deutschlands nicht verlasst, erwartet Euch ein hartes Los.» Im ersten Weltkrieg hat Bulgarien als erster von Deutschlands Verbündeten kapituliert.

90 TONNEN BOMBEN IN DER MINUTE AUF BRAUNSCHWEIG

Am 14. Januar um 7 Uhr abends unternahm die RAF einen Angriff auf das Flugzeugindustriezentrum Braunschweig, das schon am 11. Januar Ziel eines Tagesangriffes gewesen war (s Rückseite). Innerhalb 23 Minuten wurden 2000 Tonnen Bomber abgeworfen, d.h. durchschnittlich fast 90 Tonnen in der Minute. Das Tempo des Bombenabwurfs betrug bei dem RAF Angriff auf Frankfurt a/M vom 20. Dezember durchschnittlich 70 Tonnen in der Minute (Gesamt - Bombenlast: 2000 Tonnen); bei den Angriffen auf Berlin vom 2. und 16. Dezember 50 Tonnen in der Minute (Gesamt-Bombenlast jeweils 1500 Tonnen); bei dem Angriff auf Hamburg vom 24. Juli 46 Tonnen in der Minute (Gesamt-Bombenlast 2300 Tonnen).

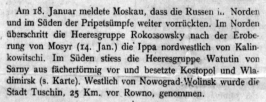

Frontpost, a weekly paper for German soldiers – it reads: 'Breakthrough to the West at the Pripet Marshes (in Russia).'

But repatriation went very slowly, because as you know, Germany was sectioned. there was the Eastern zone, French, British and American zones. The guys who'd come out of the American zone were repatriated first, then the British. I'd been called up in the Russian zone, and according to them that's where all my documentation was, so I had to go back there. Those repatriated to the east went last, but nobody bloody wanted to go in any case! They sent us back to a transit camp in Belgium — and that was worse than in Russia. There were too many people for the camps, and we really had some rough times there. I can never forgive the people for the hardship — how can I put it? It was not caused by the British or the Yanks, but by our own administration. Stuff which was coming from the Red Cross, food, never came through to us. We had no outside help. Everybody was on rations in those days — we accepted that, but when some bugger creams the top off... We were starving. We were just living in the ground, with a tent. The weather was bad, and if you said you were cold, they'd say, "Well, just dig a hole in the bloody ground."

So I decided to fly the coop. It was nothing elaborate like you see on television — I just got through the barbed wire. It wasn't hard. There were too many prisoners, and just two little Belgian kids to look after us. You'd be surprised, for a pair of boots and a couple of nice Yankee blankets, they'd even lift the barbed wire up for you, some of them... others would stick a bayonet up your arse! But we didn't get very far, and were recaptured, my friend and I. Then it was 28 days in the detention camp, everything on the double, and when we got back to the camp we'd scarpered from, the camp commander said, "Well, every POW is entitled to escape — but just forget about it, be patient." He was a nice bloke — an English major. But we escaped again, and the first washing line we came across, we lifted a couple of pairs of trousers to get out of our POW uniforms. We got a little bit further and then we got caught again.

This time the commander decided to send us to where we wouldn't escape from — and sent us to the West Country. They still had Italian prisoners of war there, and when they were repatriated, we took their place. It was a nice camp, but there were 1500 people there. Out of that, the commander picked 15 of us — my friend and I included — to go up to the camp office — we didn't know why. It turned out that we were to be billeted out on a farm — taking the place of the Italians there. With us, he was treading very gently — he tried fifteen out first, and if we behaved ourselves, he'd obviously let more out. In other words, the welfare of the camp depended on our best behaviour. Everyone wanted to be billeted out on a farm. Then the commander looked at the records of my mate and I — we'd still kept our pay books, and each time we'd stepped over the line in the army, it had been noted there. And we had an identical record of escape attempts! But he said, "I'm not changing my mind. You can go out to the farm."

It was a lovely billet. I could always speak good English, but when I went out there I pretended I couldn't understand very much. The farmer was good, but his son, who was about sixteen, he was a prize prat. He was always on about the war. He'd creep up on me with a shotgun, and say "Rudolf – Hands hoch!" There was probably nothing in it, but I told my boss in my bad English that I didn't like it. One day I was chopping wood with an axe, and I could feel the bugger creeping up on me. He came up behind the shed, and said "Hands Hoch!" And I actually heard him pulling the gun hammers back. And I thought – 'oh my God, not that.' I spun around and I let go with that fireman's axe. It went through the shed – he was behind it, at the corner, and it just missed him. He went white. He dropped the gun. I couldn't stand any more, and I chased him into the cowshed yelling at him in perfect English. There was a big box with a lid where the cowmeal was kept. I opened the box and threw him inside, closed the lid and turned the box over. When he came out he went around the village saying I was a German spy who spoke perfect English! He tried to convince everybody – but nobody believed him. I explained to them – I'm a good listener, and that way I learnt fast!

SAM NIRENBERG

I was born in a town called Dzialoszyce in Poland, in 1923. Even before the war we were poor – I won't say very poor, but we were poor. My father worked on the railway as a porter. I had four sisters and one brother. So with eight of us in all it was a struggle, but Jewish life was excellent in Dzialoszyce. It was an Orthodox town, and our education was perfect. My little town had about fourteen to fifteen thousand Jewish citizens.

My Father was a good religious man, as were all the family – well everybody was. On Friday night we used to have dinner like we have it here today. We never had plenty, but if there were any poor people who didn't have anything to eat, my father used to take them home with us. That was Polish life before the war.

Mr Niremberg in the army

There was anti-semitism before the war, but we lived together and I don't remember it having a great effect on me. I wasn't big enough to know about a lot of it. I saw it though. I saw it in 1933 when Hitler came to power and we could see what was coming. The anti-semitism got much worse then. About a month or two months before the war broke out we could see German planes flying over Poland, dropping parachutes. They were dropping spies all over the place. They made their propaganda, telling everyone to leave their towns. That's the way they carried on. What could we do? We couldn't fight, we didn't have anything to fight with!

When the Germans invaded, they started shooting people. They made everyone put all the jewellery, all the silver, all the gold and the diamonds in the middle of the market and they confiscated everything straight away. You couldn't move anywhere because Jews weren't allowed on the trains. That was the beginning.

They took us away every day to do different work, although we still lived at home then. Digging the roads, cleaning the roads, cleaning the railway station, clearing the snow. Whatever they wanted you to do you had to go out and do it. At that time it was just the able-bodied men, not the women. My father couldn't do it, he was too old. My brother was called up by the Polish army in 1939 and I never saw him again.

In about 1940 things began to get much worse. They took away the able men and made them work away from their homes. I was taken to Krakow Kobiezyna. We were digging a river there by the name of Wilga, the river goes into the Wisla. We worked deep in water. The life was very hard, but we were still able to walk around a bit – we still had a little bit of freedom. We used to go down to the Jewish ghetto in Krakow, and they used to give us a bit of food every day, then we'd carry back the buckets of food on our shoulders.

In 1941 my mother, three of my sisters and my brother's fiancee went to Belz in Poland – straight into the gas chamber. I never saw them any more. We had hidden the second youngest of my sisters, Temcha, with a Polish friend. When they evacuated the town where we lived, my father was taken to Krakow Kobiezyna, but he was unable to work and managed to get back to see how Temcha was. She had been killed, and our belongings stolen. Then he was taken to a ghetto in Radomsk and I never heard from him again. From the whole of my family only myself and three of my cousins survived. They were transported from Krakow Plaszuw to Auschwitz. They live in Israel now.

In about 1942 they took us to the concentration camp at Krakow Plaszuw and we stayed there till about 1943. Krakow Plaszuw was a terrible camp. Every day they used to bring in Polish people, not necessarily Jews either, and just kill them. Took them in the corner and just shot them. We dug the graves and covered them up. We didn't know if it was going to be us next. When they broke up the Jewish ghetto in Krakow they brought in fifty thousand people. They were all wiped out. We dug the graves and we didn't know if we'd be in them ourselves. We had a "Jude", an arm band that had our nationality on it. So they knew who we were and what we were. We had roll calls every day to see if anyone had disappeared. Everyone had a number, and they'd call the numbers out. If anyone died, or was killed, they made sure they knew. We had to carry back the people who died so they knew whom to cross off on the register.

We used to go out to work for German firms, making roads and that sort of work, and one fellow from my group escaped. We came back to the camp and they made us all walk round the Appell Platz square where roll calls were taken, a big square like a football field, and they took out every third person. One, two, three – out. One, two, three – out. Every third one they took in the corner and shot. Hundreds and hundreds and hundreds at a time. That was our punishment because one escaped. Then they brought in a lot of Jewish girls who had been hiding using Christian papers. We thought they would be better treated than us. We didn't know what the Germans would do to them. We must have dug their graves. We had to bury them and many of them were still alive. Many died like that. When they brought in people from the Jewish ghetto and shot them, more than half were still alive when they were buried. Its unbelievable what they did. I remember it as if it was today.

When I was in Krakow Plaszuw we were taken out to the railway stations to unload the Germans who had come back from the Russian front. You've never seen anything like it. They were often without feet, without noses, without ears. There were trains and trains of them all the time. We were being watched, so we couldn't walk about, but some of the Germans working on the railway used to give us things on the quiet. A bit of soap, a bit of bread, an apple. Not everyone was bad.

Then in 1943 I was one of six thousand Poles who were taken to Mauthausen in Austria. It was the middle of winter, and for the first fortnight they made us walk round naked. After all that they even looked in your mouth and up your nose – to see if you had any diamonds or anything. We walked round naked, we had nothing, what could we have hidden? Half of the Poles died from pneumonia. From Mauthausen they took able people to do work. I was put into Guzen 1, which was a Messerschmitt factory. After that they put me into Guzen 2 and we used to go round the Alps building new Messerschmitt factories for the Germans. If you couldn't carry on anymore and you came back to the camp, the next minute you were in the gas chamber. There were gas chambers in Guzen 1 and Mauthausen. They didn't give us anything to eat while we were working. We ate whatever we could find – leaves and potato peelings, mostly. We'd even eat the soft coal we found in the mountains. People used to get diarrhoea, and come home and die if they ate too much of it. Scraping around was the only thing that kept me going. In the camps the capos (section heads of prisoner groups) would often demand your bread, and if you didn't give it to them, they used to hit you to pieces.

I was only about five or six stone by the time I was in Guzen 2, but God gave me strength to carry on. I was a lucky one and I survived. There were a lot of times when

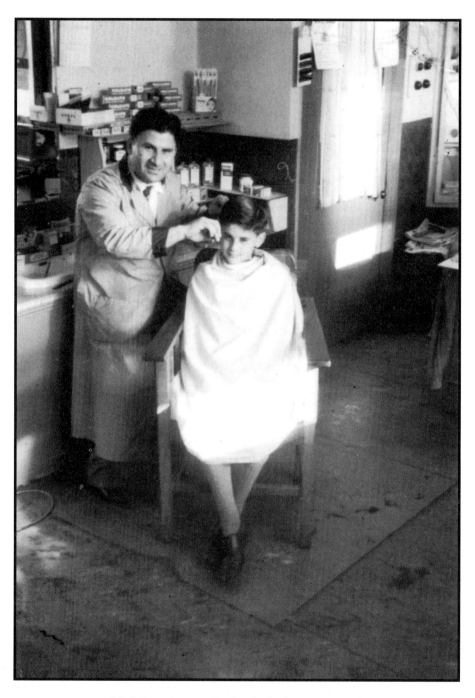

Mr Niremberg in his barber's shop in Bristol.

CHAPTER 7 – FROM EUROPE TO THE WEST COUNTRY

I was very low and felt as if I couldn't carry on. A lot of times you'd think – 'what are we living for?' We didn't know whether we were alive or dead. If the Germans did a little better on the Russian Front, they looked after us a little bit better in the camp. If they were in trouble they would give us nothing to eat. In Krakow Plaszuw I was still constitutionally strong. The weakness started in Mauthausen and I got weaker and weaker as I went to Guzen 1 and Guzen 2. I could see myself fading away completely. You saw those around you unable to walk properly, their faces and legs like those of a skeleton. Not only me but hundreds and thousands like me. You had to keep going, because if you stopped you were finished. You knew if you stopped work you would be taken to the Krankenhaus (hospital), but if you went in there you would not come out alive.

I was shot three times in Krakow Plaszuw, but if I had gone down they would have given me another one to finish me off. It was like that. The commander would come along on a horse with two pistols and just shoot at people. Not only him, they all did the same. We were a target, all of us working there – we were just targets. It was terrible. In the middle of the night the capos would wake you and say that they had to finish off a certain number of people. They chose who they wanted. Then they used to take them from their beds, drown them in a barrel of water for five minutes, then put them in the gas chamber for good measure. That's the way they used to wipe you out.

We had toilets and wash basins in the camps where you could go and have a bath or a shower. In Poland that was ok, but in Guzen you didn't know whether you would be gassed or not. They asked you to go and have a shower and the next minute you were in the crematorium. You had to go, but nobody knew who was going to the gas chamber. We didn't see the people being transported to the gas chamber in Guzen like they did in Auschwitz, but God knows how many people were brought there every night from different camps. Then they'd just burn them, burn and burn them. They were piled up all over the camp, mountains of people. About a fortnight before the liberation, in Guzen, my uncle and cousin couldn't carry on any more and they went to the wire and electrocuted themselves.

We worked until the last minute of the war. We didn't know that the war was ending, but we could sense something, because they started to take out a lot of German political people and journalists from the concentration camps and put them into the army. They were desperate for men. The guards used to be young SS men, but towards the end we were left with only the very old SS guards. We could see something was going wrong because they could only leave the old men of sixty or seventy years old. But they were just as cruel. The hardest time for me was the last few weeks before the liberation in 1945, when we walked from Guzen 2 to Gurskirchen. There were about twelve thousand Hungarian Jews and four hundred Polish Jews left. Within a week there were only about three hundred to four hundred people alive, no more than that. They wanted to finish us off completely. They had all been poisoned with soup, anyone who ate the soup was finished. It was the worst thing you could watch. There were only three huts and the people were just dying away, piling up on the floor. We felt like we were dead ourselves.

People ask, how could you lie on dead people? But we didn't know that we were lying on anybody – we didn't know anything by that point. When the Americans got to the camp they had to turn people over to see who was alive. They took me to a hospital in a little town in Austria called Wels. They tried to give me a blood transfusion but for the first two or three months they couldn't find my veins. I was just bones.

We didn't even really feel relief. We didn't know, if we had survived, we didn't know anything. A lot of people died even after the liberation because they had pneumonia. It was still a hard fight to survive. After about seven or eight months I developed some strength, but at first I couldn't even eat. From Wels we went down to Salzburg where we met the Jewish Brigade and they took us to Italy. We went to several more refugee camps, but we couldn't stand it any more so I and about seven other Jewish boys joined the Polish army. I couldn't do anything else, where could I go? I couldn't go to Palestine, or to Poland.

I survived a little bit better with the Polish army. I came over to England with them to be demobbed in September 1946. When I came here first I was in Cirencester, in the Darlingworth camp. We were still building ourselves up. I wasn't constitutionally strong but I got better because I played a lot of sport. From there they took us to another camp near Salisbury, it was called the Fargo camp. Then we went to a camp in Brockley. That was my last camp, and from Brockley I went to Didcot to get civilian clothes and get demobbed.

After being demobbed I went to Southend. I met my cousin there and she introduced me to my wife's uncle. He gave me a letter for me to go and see his brother in Bristol, and that's the way I met my wife and ended up in Bristol. I've been here ever since. I got engaged that September and we were married in December. When I was first demobbed I worked on building sites, but I couldn't really cope with the heavy work, so I trained to be a gentlemen's hairdresser. I set up my own business which is still going strong! I'm very happy here, the people were very kind to me when I first came over. I'm very satisfied – I've built up my little business and although I'm semi-retired I'm still working. Its a lovely country.

During the war I'd lived for survival. My faith did help keep me going, but I didn't really realise it at the time. I was liberated on May 4, 1945. I call it my anniversary. I've always believed in God and I believe that's the reason for what I'm doing now for the community. I go to the Synagogue in Bristol, and I do what I can to help. My nerves are ok now. I do still have nightmares – I always dream that the Germans are going to take me, and they are going to kill me. I had the same nightmare last night. Some nights I jump a foot in my bed! People just don't understand. I live with what happened and you have to get on with it. But I am very glad, very pleased to be able to talk about it. A lot of people don't understand it, but they should know a little bit of it. It's nice. Nice to be here and to be a free man.

MR AND MRS VANZELOTTI

I went with the Italian army to Tripoli, but I didn't fight. I repaired the telephone communications. The English artillery fire would break the lines, so that one department lost contact with the other. I used to go along the lines and repair them, right among the heavy fighting and underneath the bombs flying from one side to the other.

Then we made a successful offensive at Tobruk amidst such heavy fighting that the sky was red with fire. We fought across the deserts of North Africa, the Italians and Germans each fighting their own battles against the British. One day we saw soldiers coming towards us, in the distance. We thought it was the English, and fired a warning salvo. There was no response, so we launched into battle against them. It was only when they waved the surrender flag that we discovered we were fighting the Germans on our side.

We pursued the English to El Alamein, which is where we were stopped by a betrayal. One or two of our generals swapped sides and joined the English during the night. General Italobarbo was giving away our positions to the English from his aeroplane, which left us defenceless. Then the Italian navy, which had made for the port of Tobruk, shot him down out of the sky and killed him. But it was too late for us. The English gained reinforcements, and the Americans invaded Tunisia. Then there was such a battle at El Alamein as I will never forget in all my life. The English destroyed almost all the German and Italian divisions, pushing us back to Tunisia where we were scattered and finally all captured. The English had been dropping leaflets out of their planes which said: "Italians! We don't want to kill you! Surrender your arms!" So we were demoralised – why should we fight men we had never even seen?

The English asked us whether we wanted to go as prisoners with them, or with the Americans. We chose the English, because we had heard nasty stories about the way prisoners had been treated by the Americans. We sailed in convoy to England, and were bombed again by the Germans, who knew there were prisoners of war on the ships. However, we survived and disembarked at Glasgow. But the English treated us with honour. In the POW camps they allowed us baths, disinfectant, new clothes, and as much food as we wanted.

I was then taken to Easton Grey camp, near Chippenham, where we were set to work at Devizes Castle, which was an American camp. We cleaned billets, worked in the sawmills at Batheaston, on farms, clearing ditches and rivers. The work was nice, and everybody was good to us. But we were co-operative, and didn't try to escape. We used to work harder than the English!

The English, who were on rations, would come to the castle and stand in queues waiting for us to come out. We'd give them bread, tinned fruit, corned beef, coffee – everything – out of our rations. We had plenty, and this made us very popular. After a while, we were asked which of us wanted to collaborate on the English side during the war. Many refused, because it would have meant factory work. But it also meant freedom – in the evenings you could go out with plenty of girls in Bath! Those who refused had no freedom at all, so I agreed to collaborate, and became an engineer. I did anything. At night we went out, to the pictures and into the pubs. Nobody could object, although some locals were against it.

Mrs Vanzelotti:

When they were working in Devizes, they used to go out working on the farms. And they used to weave a lot of baskets, and sell them when they went out. Then they started pinching brass water taps, cut them to make wedding rings, polished them up

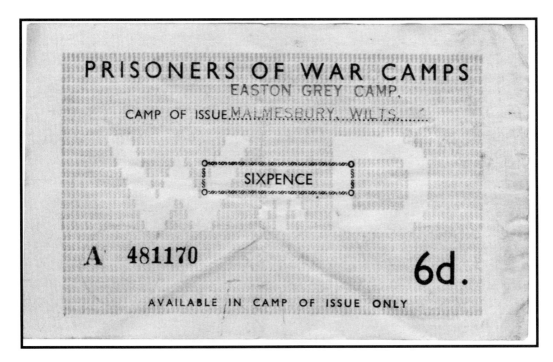

Mr. Vanzellotti's prison camp card.

and sold them to the Americans! And the Americans would send them to their wives and girlfriends. Then they would get half-crowns, and make them into cigarette lighters and brooches. Really crafty! But it was lovely work, that they did. They were very popular.

Mr Vanzelotti:

My camp commander asked us who wanted to go to work on local farms. I volunteered, because I liked the freedom of the outdoors. I was sent to this family who had no son or daughter. There was only the husband, wife and the wife's mother. I'd be fetched by him in the morning, and be brought back at night. One day he asked me if I wanted to stay and live with them. I said yes! The camp commander said it was beyond his power to grant this, and that my boss would have to write to the Home Office. So he did this, and they gave their permission. I stayed with them for years, and was treated like a son. The old mother said, "Look Emilio, if you are good and do what you're told, one day you'll be well off." Then they asked me to change my name, but I said I couldn't do that, although I would still treat them like a son would. My mother came over to visit, and my boss said to her: "You're not going to take my son away?" And she said no, she wouldn't. After years passed, the mother-in-law died, the husband, and finally the wife, who left me the whole farm – fifty acres, two houses the machinery and £1000.

Meanwhile, a friend of mine said that an Italian girl had come to work on the land in Chippenham. It turned out to be two girls, and we made friends with them, and finally got married.

Mrs Vanzelotti:

My first impression of him was doubtful, because he was from Calabria in the south, and we were from the north, near Parma. There's some friction between north and south in Italy! I had come to England as a contract worker, when I was seventeen, because there was no work at home. Everyone thought I was mad to leave my country. But I came here for six months initially – and if I had had the money to go back, I would have gone back straight away! The language was the main problem, but we were lucky because I went into the home of a commander as a private cook. There was another Italian girl there. They were really wonderful to me. His wife used to try to learn Italian by the book, so that she could communicate with us. We had a lot of laughs, between us trying to speak English and her Italian!

Because the Commander went to every part of the world he was used to continental food. Their son was in South Africa, and he would send parcels. So we managed to cook in the Italian way. My husband (who was my boyfriend then), with his friend, used to come up and have a meal with us – he'd bring the chicken and the eggs! After the first six months, I got used to the climate and the language, and things were not too bad.

I had spent the war in Italy, and saw many bad things. The north had the worst of it, because that was where the industry was. Many people were massacred. When the German soldiers heard that the Allied invasion force had landed, they hid themselves all over the countryside. We were surrounded by them – in ditches, barns... whenever they heard a noise or encountered a vehicle, they would shoot, no matter who it was. My family was shut up in a pigsty, hiding there with another family for five months. We had nowhere else to go. Our house was by the main road and the railway – it was always under attack with bombs. So we had to leave. But we could hardly move out of that pigsty, only from shelter to shelter. At first we would work for the Germans in return for food, but when the SS arrived, they wouldn't give us anything.

I have forgotten a lot of things, but I can't forget about the war. I remember everything, every step. One night – I was nine years old – there were six of us, and we were
hungry. We had to do something about it. Stupid fools were were, but when you're
young... so we crawled from our hiding place to where the Germans were asleep in
their lorries, to get the scraps they had thrown away. If we had been caught, we would
have been shot. We knew that. So whatever we found, we just picked it up and off we
went. Six journeys we did that night, because we were all so hungry.

When the Germans were forced to retreat they were killing anybody in sight. They
thought that the Italians had betrayed them, so if they saw someone talking to someone else, they thought we were sending messages. They'd come and take your brother,

Mr and Mrs Vanzellotti on their wedding day.

your father, your sister, put them against a tree or a wall, and shoot them. They weren't so bad at first, but that's how they were at the end. It was dreadful.

My youngest brother was fighting with the partisans in the mountains outside Parma. They ambushed the Germans, and Fascists who were giving them help, whenever they could. My eldest brother was also wanted and had to run away. He hid for three weeks up a tree. A farmer helped him, although he couldn't take him into the house. If he had been caught in that house, they would have shot the whole family. We knew one family with five brothers. The Germans took them and buried them all alive, up to their necks, alongside the road. Nobody was allowed to help them. No water. Nothing. We were made to keep walking past, so that we could see and would not forget what would happen to us if we worked against the Germans.

By then we had moved from the pigsty to a farm nearer the main road, so we could find out more about what was going on. We just wanted to go back to our own home. We heard that the English and Americans were coming nearer, and we saw the Germans getting in their lorries and driving off like mad. The few that were left behind hid in ditches, any place they could find so they wouldn't get caught. When we realised that the Americans were near, we split on them – "Look! There are some over there, some in that wood!" Most of them were caught. It was a small village, and a barrier was put around it, and that way about six thousand German prisoners were caught until the Americans took them away.

The villagers didn't avenge themselves – they let the Americans and English do what they wanted. My father could have killed more than one, but my mother said, "Just leave them. They're going to be punished anyway." They had taken my father, you see, because they were driving beef cattle to the Front and so took brothers, fathers, whoever they could find, to help with this. My father got to Piacenza, and luckily enough he had a cousin there who helped him to escape. He came back about three weeks later. We expected we would never see him again, because none of those who were taken came back, not even after the war.

When we heard Mussolini had been killed in Milan, we were pleased and thought, "The tyrant is dead, perhaps now the war will end." That was the reason, rather than Mussolini himself. Although he deserved it in one way, because he ruined Italy, he did a lot for the north but nothing for the south.

MRS WEBBER

I was born in Dusseldorf, in Germany, and my name was Isobel Schneider. I don't remember much about living in Dusseldorf, but I do remember people calling at us 'Jew, Jew, Jew', and children spitting at us in the street. I remember it wasn't all bad, there were a few happy times, but at the same time, you knew that you were Jewish. I remember one time I had a really nice dress made by an uncle who was a tailor, and a girl threw an orange at me and ruined the dress. My mother went to the parents of the girl and they were horribly abusive to her, saying 'Jew, Jew, Jew, go back to Palestine where you belong' and all that sort of thing. We lived with my mother because my father had left when I was about two or three to go to Spain. I really don't know what he was doing there or what sort of relationship he had with my mother, although they did correspond, I remember. He did try to contact me after the war and get me to move to Spain, but of course he was a total stranger to me by then, so I didn't go. It was my father's second marriage and the first family were much older, and my eldest half sister had taken the other children from the first marriage with her and emigrated to Israel. I think she resented my mother.

We were deported from Dusseldorf in 1938 because my mother or father were Polish by birth, either one or both, I'm not sure. It happened that the Gestapo came one particular night when my brother and I were asleep. My mother woke us up and we had to go just as we were, more or less as we stood. My mother dressed us in several layers of clothing and just took what she could and away we went. We didn't know where we were going at that stage. It was October or November 1938; we were put into prison in Dusseldorf for a couple of nights. I remember that quite clearly because it was so terrifying. Then we were all herded together and put into trucks and transported to Poland with a lot of other people. There were a lot of Gestapo with guns to make sure we didn't try to escape or anything. We came across the border and we were put into a sort of transit camp. As it turned out for us, we had relatives there: my mother had two sisters living there and one brother. I suppose they'd been alerted that we were coming and so the brother took in my mother and myself, but he had three children so they couldn't fit my brother in as well, so he was left in the camp. My mother and I lived with them. I was eight then and my brother was only seven. We saw him as much as we could at the camp. We were there from October to the following August, and then it was obvious that war was coming and they tried to get as many children out as they could. I was one of those lucky ones who got out. I nearly didn't because

I'd caught some kind of fever and I was in hospital, but I just managed to get well enough to come across. My brother was left behind in the camp. I don't know why I was chosen to come on the Kindertransport and not my brother, but it might be that I was stronger than him. I remember hearing from my mother while I was still waiting to go that he was very ill and maybe had whatever I had. Other children who came across also had brothers and sisters left behind. Perhaps they could only take a quota from each family. Of course I wonder now about what my mother must have gone through, making these decisions. You think about these things, especially when you have children of your own.

I had a couple of cards and a letter from my mother while I was in the hospital, but I never heard from her again once I came over here. I suppose it was because we were the last boat out and there wasn't any contact possible once the war started.

I don't remember what the illness I had was, but I remember being on a special diet, and I must have been in partial isolation even when I came over because I don't remember seeing many other children on the voyage. When we had a reunion of Kindertransport children in 1988, there was a lady who could remember my brother in that camp. Of course they all went in the end: my mother, my brother, my aunties and uncles and cousins. They were all killed in the camps.

We arrived in London and we were all dispersed into different families. I was put in with another girl who'd come over with me. But it was so near the start of the war, within a week we were on our way again.

Of course we couldn't speak English, which was difficult because when I came to Sheldon, near Dunkerswell in Devon. The girl I'd come across with and I were billeted with two other English girls, on this Irish lady whose husband was in the navy. It was very difficult for us because we couldn't communicate with them. We went to a Jewish school. They separated the school so that there was the English speaking side and us. The Jewish teachers who were evacuated with us hadn't come across on the transport with us and so they had no idea what sort of trauma we were going through. They were Jewish teachers, but they were English, so in a lot of ways they couldn't identify with us at all.

The Irish lady had a cat which was allowed on the table when there was food around and so the two older, English girls reported this and then we were separated again so we were eating at one place and sleeping at another. That wasn't so good, so me and

CHAPTER 7 – FROM EUROPE TO
THE WEST COUNTRY

Salma, the girl that came over with me, were billeted at the vicarage. There were teachers billeted there as well, and although we didn't understand a lot of what was going on, we knew there was quite a lot of friction. Children sense these things.

Some of the children went back to their parents after a while and so they decide to move me to Tallerton. Salma, had come over with her brother but he was in another part of the country, and she went to him and they went to relatives in Canada. I landed up at Tallerton and I stayed there until I got married. I was put with a couple who had no children and I called them Auntie and uncle. They wanted to adopt me, but again I said no. Really, I was spoiled there, they were such a lovely couple. I always kept in contact with them as they were the nearest thing to family for me. I finally had some security, but even then gradually the teachers went back and there were only four Jewish children left in the village. Two sisters, a boy and myself. The Jewish organisations felt that being billeted with gentiles wasn't right, so they kept on hounding us, telling us to pack up and be ready at such and such a date, we're coming to collect you and so on. We had that to contend with because they hadn't a clue really as to what we'd been through and how for the first time for ages we'd found some kind of security. You can understand how they felt, but they kept hounding us. In the end we were about twelve or thirteen, they realised they'd have to drag us out screaming so they gave up on us. They sent a teacher out from Exeter once a week to try and teach us Hebrew. I could have learnt it quite easily but I just shut myself off, so eventually that stopped too. Much later I realised that they had only been trying to keep us in the faith; perhaps even out of respect for our own parents, they felt it a duty, but it's just a pity they went about it the wrong way. Since then I've become a Christian, but that was a decision I made much later in life.

Then the boy found out that his mother and sister had escaped and were in London, so he went off to be united with them. I think they'd escaped through Russia and come over. That left just the three of us in the village. Then I met Ken, my husband, when I was seventeen, and got married at eighteen. The other two girls got married too, one to a local man and the other to someone working at the post office who later became a vicar. I still keep in touch with them.

I did find out later that one of my aunties had escaped from Germany and was living in England, and that I've got two cousins here. Later on, when she did get in contact, she wanted to adopt me as I found out years afterwards, but at that time I'd really settled and I could remember my own mother, so I didn't want to be adopted. About the time I got engaged to Ken, they cut me off, which is of course what Jewish people do if you intend to marry out of the faith. At first I didn't realise they'd cut contact with me, I just wondered why I didn't hear from Auntie Freda any more, but that's what it was. Anyway, I didn't hear from them for years until their own daughter married out of the faith, and after that my Auntie contacted me again. They cut her off for a time until she had children and then they were reconciled again.

I don't speak any German now. You must remember, it was war time when I came over and as far as I was concerned, the sooner I forgot German, the better. Of course maybe if I'd had others to speak to I'd have kept it up, but anything in connection with Germany was taboo over here.

MRS WILKS

I was fourteen when the war started. It was September 1st, 1939, and I was going to school when the bombs started falling on Warsaw. We saw the planes going over and thought – oh, they're our planes! But they were German Stukas. It was jet black, and it seemed as if the heavens opened with the Germans bombing Warsaw, before they even declared war. So we kids ran back home, and there was my mother running to the window putting pillows up, thinking the Germans were going to throw gas – because she had lived through the First World War.

Then the Germans walked into Poland. It was 24th September. We put barricades up, but nothing stopped them. We hoped that the Russians would help us, but the Russians attacked us from the east. Our army wasn't very big, or strong, because Poland was only nineteen years old – a new country. We had been occupied for 150 years. We didn't have a large enough army to fight on two fronts. They sent the Polish cavalry with sabres against the German tanks! Anyway, our government ran away to England. There was only the mayor of Warsaw who was a Polish hero, and stayed to the end. He was executed by the Germans. They shot him for being in the Resistance.

There were two German soldiers killed in Warsaw, so they took some hostages, and executed them. A couple of weeks after, some more Germans were killed in Warsaw, so they burned a whole village outside Warsaw. They surrounded the whole village, took

Mr and Mrs Wilks

all the livestock out – chickens, pigs – and started burning the houses. So all the people ran to the church – for protection, I suppose – and the Germans set the church on fire with a flame-thrower. And any people who ran away from the burning church, they machine-gunned them. That place is still as it was when the Germans burned it. It's left as a memorial to the dead.

1940 came, and we had two underground movements. The Socialist Party, and the Peasant Army – Communists. They got on all right together. One fought the Germans and one the Russians.

You couldn't get food. You saw people breaking into shops, pinching what they could. You couldn't buy bread, potatoes, nothing. You couldn't get anything for a sack of gold. There were some horses opposite us. We used to go over to them, when the Stukas had finished bombing. The artillery opened fire at night time – twenty-four hours a day, and the horses were killed. We'd go and cut a piece of horse flesh, because we had nothing to eat.

Up in the ghetto – it was dreadful. I can't speak about it. The English don't understand what it's like to be under occupation. If I were to be occupied again by the Germans, or the Russians, I would commit suicide. I saw a mother climb to the fifth floor of a building with her children, and throw them out of the window, and then jump out herself, because she couldn't stand it any more under the Germans.

You were not allowed to have a radio. There was one radio in the whole street. One person – nobody knew who it was, or which house – listened to London and the news would pass around from mouth to mouth. There was a death penalty for having a radio. We had great big loudspeakers on every lamp-post, and the Germans would broadcast their propaganda through the radio to us – the English got bombed, and France... you know. We listened to London – everybody waiting for the latest news – but who had that radio? Nobody knows to this day. Victory signs appeared on the houses, and in the parks. The Germans didn't like that, but who was doing it?

I was a churchgoer. You know what Catholics the Poles are! But the Germans didn't like us going to church. That church in Warsaw was not in the centre of the town, but on a traffic island, in the middle. It was a beautiful church. The Germans surrounded that church; and everybody in it, even the priest, was taken in the lorry, and sent to the assembly place where they kept people and sorted them before they sent them to Germany, to the concentration camps. And that's how I came to be sent to Germany. My mother and niece followed afterwards.

There was only me, and my mother, and my two brothers. One brother managed to escape from the Germans, but my elder brother was injured in the defence of Warsaw. He gave himself up – because he was an officer – and was sent to the POW camp in Germany – to Dachau. The Germans didn't treat other prisoners of war as they treated the English or Americans. To them he was a Pole, and they tried to finish the Poles as they tried to finish the Jews. But he survived the war and was sent to Belgium. I received a letter from him, but I never saw him again after 1939, because he was in hiding.

When I arrived in Germany, they put us into Arbeitsdienst – like a labour exchange. We stood in a line – like a cattle market – and the Germans, and farmers, would come along and choose who they wanted for work. They never chose town people for farm

Mrs Wilks' marriage certificate.

work – they took them to factories, or as private servants. First I was sent to a private house. A German woman chose me – Frau Oliverts. She was very nice to me. Her husband was in a concentration camp – he got drunk and he called Hitler a nasty name – so in the night the Gestapo came and sent him away, for nine, ten months. So he hated the Nazis: and in his house, he had a picture, and on one side was a picture of Hitler, and on the other, Kaiser Wilhelm. If anybody was going to be shocked he turned the picture around to Hitler – if not, it was reversed! They were a very nice family. They had a son in the airforce.

But then came the order that you weren't allowed to have private workers, because they needed people in the factories. So I was sent to a factory where electric motors were made. Oh, it was hard work – for five marks a month. When I came to London I had callouses on my hands. I had to wear a yellow star, with a purple border and a purple P in the middle. I used to argue with the Germans and the police: I said, "Am I a dog to wear a label like that?" But I had to wear it. I was seventeen.

The factory got bombed, and we were supposed to get the machinery out. And again, I wouldn't, so the Gestapo got me again and sent me to a work camp on the railways near Cologne. They marched us to work, where we worked between the sleepers on the railway lines, putting the stones there. The Americans and English kept bombing the railway lines, so we had to repair it. But it wasn't long before I skedaddled from there. And I was very lucky – although it was January 1945 when I ran away. I was hiding in the woods. I would walk during the night, when people in farms – Poles – would give me food. There was such chaos then, that nobody bothered very much about prisoners – the whole camp could run away and noone would worry about it. It was March by the time the American soldiers came to West Germany and I had been hiding in the woods for three months. You don't think about the dangers when you're young. And I was very patriotic then: when I was sent back to Germany first I would have walked on my knees to get back to Warsaw.

The Americans put us in a refugee camp in Aachen, a great big SS camp. All different nationalities were there, and some Russians and Ukrainians. The Ukranians were worse to the Jews in the ghettoes than the Germans had been. When the Americans first arrived in the camp, they gave the Polish prisoners 24 hours to do what they liked with the Germans. I never saw anyone do anything, though. There used to be a death penalty for pinching the smallest thing, so I think people were still scared.

The Americans fed us, but if you wanted a cup of coffee and a dog biscuit you had to queue all night to get it – that was the only food they gave us. You can't survive on that. We were fenced in like animals, there was no freedom at all in the camp. The locals used to come and laugh at us saying, "You think things were bad when we had you, look how your friends the Americans treat you now!" They were supposed to be our allies, and they fenced us in. This Polish woman went through the fence, to get some milk for her baby, and they shot her. They only injured her, I admit, but they shot her. Towards April they sorted us out into different camps and they removed the

Russians from us, because the Poles and the Russians never see eye to eye. Even in peacetime they fight.

We knew this couple at the camp. The wife had her child taken away when the Germans were in power. She was made to give birth in a field, and when they saw that the baby was blonde with blue eyes they took the child away to a kindergarten in a German orphanage. She didn't see him again until after the war; when she finally found him he was nearly four years old. He didn't speak a word of Polish, and if any-one looked at him he'd say, "Heil Hitler!" He was a proper little German devil. The Germans took away a lot of Polish children, they just wanted their blonde hair and blue eyes. They were desperate to replace the men they had lost in the war. I am a Christian woman, but what the Germans did to us I can never forget or forgive.

We were moved to another camp and again the Americans locked us all in. It wasn't so bad there though and we had a bit of fun. We'd make a deal with the Yanks – I'd say, we'll meet you tonight, let us go out, and they'd let you go, but of course we didn't go to see them ! Some of the American soldiers were very generous, they gave us fags and chocolate, and condoms! With those you could get some food on the black market.

The camp was filthy. They used the same room for sleeping and as a toilet. There were forty of us in one room, like pigs. No water, no electricity. We used to take it in turns to keep the room clean and when it was my turn my fiancé used to carry the water for me. I was ever so tiny – I was only six stone!

When the English came and took over from the Americans the first thing they did was take the wire down. Then there was nobody in the camp, nobody. Everybody went out – freedom – we could go out. Then at least we didn't have to be humiliated by the Germans taking the mickey out of us. That was in May 1945, just when the war finished.

Mr Wilks:

We met at the refugee camp. It must have been a Saturday or a Sunday. She was riding this bike, so I borrowed one and followed her. But there she was waiting for me, wasn't she – so I didn't stand a chance!

The thing was, I did not like darning socks so I used to use string. She didn't think this was right so she darned them all nicely with wool. My rifle was very neglected and she took it and she polished it, made a magnificent job of it. And my gear was in a state and she renovated it. Well, I mean, how could I escape?

I was working in the camp away from my battalion. There were about ten of us there, and between us we supervised all the work. I had a work party of five old men and one very old one. He was never allowed to do anything. I used to go out and get a load of cabbages to feed them. I used to detest the potato run. When I say potatoes, don't imagine what you see in the shops, these were rotten. It was all we could get. I'd take about five people from the camp, and always this kid called Eugene. He had been turned mental. He used to get a handful of this potato mush, and the others would do the same, and they'd belt it at any passing cyclist. And I used to dread it, coming along that autobahn, because it didn't matter if it was the military governor or whoever – they didn't care, and I never saw one that didn't fall off his bike!

Food was a difficult problem. The British at Bonn gave us so much, but the UNRA (United Nations Refugee Association) got hold of most of it and sold it on the German black market. We were supposed to get one Red Cross food parcel per Displaced Person every week, but only one parcel between six people would get through. They were pinching everything from all the Displaced Persons (DP) camps and the people were hungry, walking round in rags. The UNRA didn't even provide disinfectant. It didn't seem to matter what went into that UNRA store, it wasn't coming out into the camp kitchen.

The UNRA used to go out very late at night. I know that because the Germans were crafty: at night they used to fill the tram lines with sand so that the UNRA cars would get stuck, and whilst the driver went to get help they'd nick the car! Anyway, one night this happened to an UNRA bloke and he came to us for help. I reckon the crafty devil had been out selling the stuff to the Germans himself on the black market.

Mrs Wilks:

He waited three days and then he proposed to me. Funny thing is, before I met him I was friendly with his Sergeant. A Londoner – Danny Chapel. Once a week we had a band playing in the garage. That Danny Chapel he used to dance so beautifully! Eddie couldn't dance – didn't know his left from his right! But he had something, though goodness knows what!

We had a Catholic church, in the garage, in the DP camp and I wanted to get married in my faith and Eddie in his. So I went to see the Polish Padre and he said, "Oh no, I'm not doing that, you and all your children will go to Hell, doing that!" So I said, "Oh, you go to hell yourself!" That priest had been in a concentration camp, and he hadn't learnt anything. He survived, but he had no understanding.

It was coming up to Christmas 1945 by then, and they were teaching the children songs in the chapel near the camp. It was beautiful, I used to stop and listen to it. The children were practising for a big Christmas service. When the day came along the church was packed, with thousands of people. It was just starting, when one of the British staff from the camp entered the church with his German girlfriend, and ruined everything. The whole church started walking out. It stopped everything, just as if someone had shot the priest.

Mr Wilks:

So I went to see the CO. It was the Coldstream Guards you know, you had to do everything by the book. If you did, you were treated very, very well. The Padre was there, with the CO, who said, "Well, I can't stop you." I had a letter from my father saying, "If that's the way you want it, you carry on." But the Padre didn't want to know. I thought, 'if he doesn't want to know, I'll find someone who does.' The Horse Guards were stationed down at Bruehl, just south of Cologne, and so we went down there. The Padre with the Horse Guards there was a really nice gentleman, the Rev. Alexander. Before joining the Guards, he was the vicar of Henbury Parish Church in Bristol, and might still be remembered by the senior people of the parish. He was tickled because we were the first couple he was going to marry in Germany. That was in January 1946, and we were married in the castle.

Mrs Wilks:

Well, Eddie didn't want me to stay at the DP camp after we were married, so he sent me back to England, to Bristol, all by myself! And I couldn't speak a word of English. I was on the ship and I was crying my eyes out. There was a young lady in a navy uniform, a Wren I think, and she was a Bristolian. She looked after me.

It was all so strange for me, I was crying my eyes out throughout the whole journey. The RTO put me in a big truck all by myself to London Bridge when we landed at Dover. It was the first time I saw a prefab – I thought they were dolls houses, they were so tiny. I finally arrived at Shirehampton station on Saturday and his parents weren't there. While I was on my way to Bristol, his parents were coming to meet me – so we missed each other! In the end they were so worried they had the police looking for me.

Meanwhile I thought I was going to have nowhere to stay. There was this lady on the platform, and she saw what a state I was in and, you know, she took me home to her house on the Portway! I was a stranger to her, but she was so kind – she had never seen me before, but she took me into her home like that. It was fantastic. We were friends for a long time. Then I registered with a shop and I found I could have whatever I wanted! Food was supposed to be rationed, but I never knew about that – I felt like a film star! I'd give my coupons to the lady in the shop and she'd say, "What would you like, Christina?" I even had meat delivered on Saturday and Wednesday – why? – because the butcher had been in the Polish Navy! It was wonderful! Honestly, I didn't know what it was to be on rations.

I have lived in Bristol ever since, and I think the Bristolians are the kindest people I ever met. They're very reserved in the beginning, but when they get to know you, they're really good friends.

RECOMMENDED FURTHER READING

Bristol Lives
Bristol Broadsides 1987

A Boy In Your Situation   Charles Hannam
Andre Deutsch 1988

Poems of the Second World War   The Oasis Selection
Published in association with the Salamander Oasis Trust
and J.M. Dent Ltd London 1990

Shepton Mallet Camera   Fred Davis
Pub. Shepton Mallet Amenity Trust Ltd 1992

Shepton Mallet Prison   Francis Disney BEM.
Pub. by Francis Disney, Shepton Mallet 1992.

West at War   James Belsey and Helen Reid
Redcliffe Press Bristol 1990

A World Worth Fighting For   Ex-Servicemen's CND

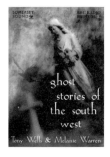
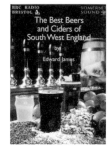